The House of
Yahweh
My Side of the Story

A riveting, tell-all memoir by the woman who was married to Yisrayl Hawkins, leader of The House of Yahweh, which came to be known as America's largest doomsday cult. Rarely do we get such a detailed account from a high-level insider. Readers will learn how such a group can go from benign to dangerous and abusive in no time, and will also better understand why so many would go along with bizarre practices while worshiping a malignant narcissist. This is an important book for anyone interested in cults, extremism or undue influence.

By Janja Lalich, Ph.D.
Professor of Sociology
Author of
Take Back Your Life: Recovering from Cults and Abusive Relationships
and *Bounded Choice: True Believers and Charismatic Cults*

The House of
Yahweh

My Side of the Story

by

Kay Hawkins

ex-wife of the Elder and Overseer

authorHOUSE®

AuthorHouse™
1663 Liberty Drive
Bloomington, IN 47403
www.authorhouse.com
Phone: 1-800-839-8640

I am grateful for the permissions that were granted to me to reprint or adapt from the works cited throughout my book.

Published by AuthorHouse 7/17/2012

ISBN: 978-1-4772-1706-1 (sc)
ISBN: 978-1-4772-1705-4 (hc)
ISBN: 978-1-4772-1704-7 (e)

Library of Congress Control Number: 2012910403

Any people depicted in stock imagery provided by Thinkstock are models, and such images are being used for illustrative purposes only. Certain stock imagery © Thinkstock.

This book is printed on acid-free paper.

Because of the dynamic nature of the Internet, any web addresses or links contained in this book may have changed since publication and may no longer be valid. The views expressed in this work are solely those of the author and do not necessarily reflect the views of the publisher, and the publisher hereby disclaims any responsibility for them.

To my daughter and sons, DeeDee Corbin, David Hawkins, and Justin Hawkins: Thank you for letting me share your stories, and for giving me excellent advice as you read the manuscript. My book would not have been the same without your counsel.

To my daughter, Margo Corneillie: Thank you for letting me share your story, and for reading the manuscript, which gave it the final polish.

To my son, Dennis: Thank you for letting me share your story and your pain.

Each of you lived these events, and you are testimony to survival and success after cult involvement.

To Ruby, and to the Leaders of the Assembly of Yahweh, 7th Day: Thank you for your advice and help.

To my sister and brother-in-law: Thank you for patiently leading me into the Twenty-First Century of technology and the wonders of the Internet.

To all of my wonderful family, friends, and associates, without you part of my story could not have been warm and delightful.

Contents

Preface

Why did people flock to The House of Yahweh, Abilene, even with all the negative publicity focused against it? They were here because they had searched for something that the churches and assemblies had not been able to offer them. At the time, The House of Yahweh had the answers they had been looking for.

I would also like to let you know that the majority of people who joined The House of Yahweh while I was there were not weird, crazy, stupid, or any other such thing. These members were owners of companies, business men and women, supervisors, construction workers, trades people, and ordinary people who went to work every day and provided for their families. You might have been working right next to one and never knew it, unless they had informed you.

The House of Yahweh made contact with prospective new members through its publishing and media enterprises. First, there were the advertisements placed in national periodicals. Some requested to be placed on our mailing list and they were sent selected booklets and the current issues of our magazine, *The Prophetic Word*.[1] Some of these people eventually came to celebrate the feasts with The House of Yahweh. One cannot just read one copy of the magazine and be considered as one of the holy family. There was a process of elimination. Those who came to the feasts and who still questioned anything, simply were not invited back.

The books published by The House of Yahweh were offered to our readers, such as: *The Mark of The Beast Vol. I* and *The Mark of The Beast Vol. II, Did Yahshua Messiah Pre-exist?, The Sabbath, Every Question Answered,* and *Devil Worship, The Shocking Facts*.[2]

People who had been searching their whole lives for understanding of the scriptures had found it in the publications they first received. Why would anyone who had been searching for this refuse to become a part of it?

During the feasts beginning in 1991, Yisrayl Hawkins remained secluded in his private office, only showing his face to preach during some of the services. The people in the audience only saw the man from afar. When they were invited into his private domain for an appointment, they were flattered. What was not understood at the time was that this was when Yisrayl Hawkins sized them up, to learn what they might be worth to him.

Each of the new members was assigned a "counselor" beginning in 1993, who carefully paced them throughout their conversion process; a process much like a child learning to walk. When they were proven to be loyal, the men were informed they had the right to take more than one wife; the women were told that in order to honor Yahweh, they must start by submitting to the authority of their own husbands.

By this time, however long it might have taken, this was no longer simply a religion. This was a part of our lives. We were also told to believe that if anyone left The House of Yahweh that they would burn in hell. Those who remained were slaves forever.

The House of Yahweh, Abilene, Texas, was a part of my life for over fourteen years. There is not a week that goes by that I do not think about the wonderful times that I experienced there. There is also not a week that goes by that I do not remember the horror and depression that I also experienced at this same place.

I want to tell you my story about The House of Yahweh, Abilene, and my experiences with Buffalo Bill Hawkins, who would eventually come to be known as Yisrayl B. Hawkins, the Elder and Overseer of this organization.

The events of our lives together framed the building of The House of Yahweh organization, and also its spiritual condition today. I have another motive for writing my account of these events. It is to clarify so many things which were spoken by Yisrayl Bill Hawkins. At the time that he was speaking, I was forced to remain silent. Now, listen to my side of the story.

CHAPTER ONE

My Story Begins

My own religious and personal experiences found me searching for roots, security, and a special church that I knew had to be out there somewhere. This would eventually bring me in contact with Buffalo Bill Hawkins. I will begin with the fact that Mother and Daddy were living with Grandmother when I was born in 1948. I have vivid memories of my grandmother, one especially profound. I remember the day that Grandmother was buried. One of the neighbors was babysitting me at home. I asked the lady where my grandmother was. She said, "She's in heaven." I asked her, "Where is heaven?" She said, "Up in the sky, and she is looking down at you right now." I did not believe her. I knew that if my grandmother was looking at me that she would come down and get me, and since she did not come get me then she did not see me. This was my first, deeply embedded, religious experience. I did not believe that anyone went to heaven when they died.

I was in the fifth grade of elementary school when I experienced the second event which would profoundly shape my religious future. Ironically, it was on the day that my class had just finished celebrating our Christmas party. There was a set of *The Encyclopedia Britannica* [3] in our classroom and, curious about the holiday, I opened one of the books to the article on "Christmas." Chills ran over me as I read the fact that the celebration of Christmas had its origin in the festival of Saturnalia in pagan Rome and not from the bible. It was at that moment that I began to question my religious training and started reading the bible for myself.

Two days after I turned eighteen, I married Kenneth Darrel Rogers. We moved to Haskell, Texas, into a small apartment. Afterward, we moved around following the oil wells. It was also during this time that I visited several different churches, searching for a congregation that worshipped on Saturday and still believed in the Messiah.

It was when we moved back to Haskell that our son, Dennis Morgan, was born in the County Hospital. Trying to make a living in the oil patch was, as my mother said, "Chicken one day and feathers the next." Because we had more feathers than chicken during the winter of '66–'67, we packed up and moved from Texas to New Mexico where a roughneck job was waiting. The oil patch then took us in the spring to Utah and then to Colorado in the fall. In December of 1968 we went back to Texas and stayed with my parents for a while. In the spring of 1969 we went back to Colorado to take up where we left off in the western oil patch. In April of 1969 Kenneth was killed in a car accident while on his first day back to work.

Dennis and I lived with my parents for a while and then moved into the Huckleberry Mobile Home Park in Abilene, Texas, where I had planned to attend college. Instead, I met Teddy Bryan Daniel. I married him and my mobile home was hauled to Stamford. We virtually partied every Saturday night. Teddy was well liked and had many friends. We had a lot of fun. In 1970 Deirdre Yvette (DeeDee) was born in Stamford Memorial Hospital. Ted quit work at the radio station and began working in a paint and body shop, and eventually became part owner of one. The partying stopped. We could barely pay our bills and then we could not pay them at all. We had borrowed money and used my car as collateral. Ted's business failed.

In the spring of 1971 I became employed at Timex Corporation in Abilene. By the fall of that year we had moved back to Abilene, back to Huckleberry Lane in order to be closer to my work. Teddy was unemployed but was searching. At the beginning of February, 1972, I found I was again pregnant. About that same time Teddy found a position with an insurance company as a salesman. His territory would be around Baird, Texas, so we were required to move there. I remained employed at Timex. Two fellow employees agreed to drive me back and forth to work each day, while Teddy took my car to work with him.

About two months after that, Teddy lost his job. He immediately left town with his first cousin to find work in San Angelo, Texas, or so he told me. It was not long afterward that I learned that Ted had also found another woman.

I was stranded in Baird, Texas, pregnant, with two children. Ted's cousin's wife was staying with me. I had about $80.00 in savings in the Timex Credit Union. I had to get back to Abilene to be closer to my job at Timex so I could save the driving fee money; and beside that, I did not know a soul here. I drove to Abilene to search for a mobile home park into which I could move.

First, I had hoped to acquire a space at a very nice park. This area had fenced lots with big trees, close to my work, with a good neighborhood for children. Upon filling out my application at the park office, I made the mistake of telling the leasing agent that another woman would be staying with me for a short time. I was refused service. The leasing agent, a female, stated, "That kind of arrangement never worked out." This was 1972 and still a white man's world. Single women with children were considered to be "bad news," so any reason to refuse service was justification enough.

On reflection later, it seemed as though I was pre-determined to cross paths with Buffalo Bill Hawkins.

After being refused occupancy in the nice park, I drove to the other trailer park which was close to Timex, "Ready Trailer Park." I drove past this place every day on my way to work. It looked like a seedy, run-down dump, but the motive for moving back to Abilene was to be closer to Timex. I went to the small rental office in the middle of the park and met Mr. and Mrs. Nathan Daugherty. Mrs. Daugherty showed me the available vacant space. It had a fenced lot, a cute little wishing well in the front, and large mesquite trees, so much nicer than the locations that fronted the street. Of course, I said nothing about anyone else but my children living with me. Ted's cousin's wife left when I filed for divorce against Teddy.

I assumed that Mr. and Mrs. Daugherty were the owners of the park. I paid the rent at their small mobile home—on time every month, but had no other interaction. My sister moved in with me shortly afterward and we shared living expenses. Dennis was staying with Mother and Daddy in Royston to help me financially and to send him to school. I was also concerned for my children's safety. I saw a police car driving through the park almost daily. I thought that there were bad things constantly going on in this neighborhood, for the police to be around so often. I never allowed my children to play outside the gate and made no acquaintances.

After I had lived there a while, I reported to the Daugherty's that my gate latch did not work. The following Saturday morning, a light teal metallic blue pickup drives up, and out steps a redneck cowboy with a peeled haircut topped off with a brown Stetson hat. He was wearing western clothes and cowboy boots. He began to work on the front gate. I told my sister that I was going out to show him what the problem was. This is how I met Buffalo Bill Hawkins for the first time. You know how they say, "love at first sight"—not in this story. It would not be until December of this same year that we would meet again.

At this point in my life I was physically and mentally exhausted. I was bearing the responsibility for supporting my family, was pregnant and living from paycheck to paycheck. I had hit bottom. Spiritually I had said to myself, "I will never again be committed to a sweet good-old-boy or to a good-looking party animal." Neither type had matched my ambition or the perseverance to succeed. I had been moving around from one place to the other since I had first married, and I wanted the same roots and security for my children that I had as a child. Only a man who would be loyal to me, and who had the ability to make something of himself in order for us to have this kind of security would ever interest me again. I had set my goal.

David Wayman, my son, was born in October of 1972 at Stamford Memorial Hospital. I had taken maternity leave from Timex Corporation, and when I was able to return there were no jobs available. I was out of work. Added to that stress was the stress of the threat of having my mobile home repossessed. I learned that Teddy had borrowed a little over $2,000.00 from a businessman in Stamford and had used my mobile home as collateral. The problem about that was that he never bothered to tell me about it. To prevent some mobile home moving truck from literally tying on to the tongue of my mobile home and carrying it away, when I moved into Ready Trailer Park I had the tires removed.

Thinking of the tires which were stored under my mobile home, I hoped to get permission to place these inside a large building located inside the park—and the time that I had available while on maternity leave was the time to act.

It was around the middle of the second week in December, 1972, that I went to the office to make this request. Mr. Daugherty said that he would ask his "boss" if that was ok. I then asked Mr. Daugherty who owned the park. He said, "Bill Hawkins." Was I surprised to learn that the corn-fed cowboy who came to fix my gate during the summer was the landlord himself.

How I Met Him

Before I continue my story, I have to furnish some background information about Buffalo Bill Hawkins. If I had known then what I know now, this story would never have occurred in the first place. The only sad thing about that would have been that I would never have had the wonderful daughter and son that I have now, and I probably would never have found that special religion that I had been searching for.

This is what I was able to learn about him, much later in time: Buffalo Bill Hawkins was born to William Otis Hawkins and Maggie Mae Russell Hawkins at 3:00 am on August 28, 1934, in Lexington, Oklahoma, Cleveland County, and according to the information on his birth certificate, he was the fourth living child of five children: J.G., Mary Bell, Margaret, Vernon George, then Bill.

It was told to me by Bill that his mother, pregnant with him, father, and siblings fled by horse and wagon to Oklahoma to be near his family after the bank foreclosed on their land.

The 1930 U.S. Census shows that Bill's father was a sharecropper who farmed someone else's land in Precinct 1, Young County, Graham, Texas. Bill must have confused this story with that of his grandfather, Lewis Daniel Hawkins, who actually did own land at one time in Denton County, Texas.[1] Whatever the true reason, the year 1929 began the Great Depression and Bill's mother and dad were among its victims.

Otis and Maggie were tough and did the very best they could under crippling conditions. Bill never seemed to realize their great struggle and sacrifice to provide for their family and keep it together. When Bill was twelve-years-old, his brother, J.G., married his wife, Isabel,[2] on June 2,

---

1   See Appendix One.
2   By request of her family, Jacob's wife's name has been changed to protect the feelings of the innocent and some of her children's privacy.

1944, her seventeenth birthday. Isabel said she and J.G. lived with Mr. and Mrs. Hawkins for several years and she was always treated well.

Bill's childhood stories revolved around his life in Lexington and Purcell, Oklahoma: His dad was a sharecropper. His mother and dad went to town in a buckboard wagon. He raised a calf that his dad sold out from under him. He nearly killed the family horse by forcing him to plow a field at double time, so he could finish the job faster and go to town. He and his brother, Vernon, hunted small animals (cats included which looked like rabbits when they were skinned, said Isabel Hawkins) and sold their carcasses (rabbits and cats, said Isabel) to the neighbors to have money in their pockets. Bill said he did not do well in school, could not focus, and dropped out of school in the fifth grade. Two brothers were born later, Texas James and Gene Truman.

On June 25, 1950, the Korean Army crossed the 38th parallel and the Korean War broke out, not ending until 1953. During this time-span, when Bill was seventeen-years-old, in 1951, he said he had a job for a short time at a gas station in Purcell. Around 1952, at age eighteen, Buffalo Bill Hawkins was married to Rosa Bell Bolding. Also beginning around 1952, Bill and J.G began studying with Herbert W. Armstrong and were affiliated with The World Church of God (later changed to The Worldwide Church of God). One of Armstrong's doctrines was that no member was allowed to serve in the armed forces. This suited J.G. and Bill just fine. Bill refused to be drafted, but accepted an assignment with the State Board of Health Laboratories in Topeka, Kansas, where he obtained much of his later sermon material.

In 1957, Bill, age twenty-three, and J.G., age thirty-three, were enrolled in Midwest Bible College, sponsored by the Church of God, Seventh Day, in Stanberry, Missouri, led by Andrew N. Dugger. Bill was living on North Maple Street.

He told me that it was so cold in Missouri that he parked his car, drained the radiator to prevent it from freezing, and walked to college. He also told me that he had rented rooms in his house to elderly people to have an income.

Bill was still married to Rosa Bell in 1957 when he was attending bible college, but it would not be too much longer before she and the college would both be replaced.

According to Bill, he was driving a cab, another of his many jobs, and that Rosa Bell had an affair with his best friend. When Bill found out, he said he packed her things and drove her back to her parents' home and left her; that he never heard from her again.

Isabel Hawkins told a different story, saying that Bill started performing in a rock band and met Dena[3] in a night club. Bill soon learned that Dena had access to her own money and she helped Bill promote his singing career. It was Bill who began having the affair. When Rosa Bell learned about it she confronted Bill. He packed some of his clothes and moved in with Dena. Bill never took Rosa Bell back to her parents, Isabel explained, because she was raised in an orphanage and did not even know them.

In April of 1961, Buffalo Bill Hawkins was living in Graham, Texas, with Dena and her son. Bill said he worked at the Graham Flour Mill, as did his father, Otis Hawkins, who was raising his two youngest sons by himself. Maggie, Bill's mother, had passed away in 1956. J.G. Hawkins and his family would also move to Graham, Texas, to be close to their family around this time. Three of Bill and Dena's daughters were born between 1961 and 1964.

Bill held small jobs from 1950 to 1961—worked at a gas station, worked at a poultry plant, sold bibles door to door, worked at a concrete company driving a concrete truck, performed in a rock band, worked for a State Highway Department, where he said his supervisor, whom he hated, forced his crew to work indoors during nice weather and outdoors in severe weather, where Bill contracted a case of pneumonia and was forced to quit his job. Bill worked at the Graham Flour Mill from 1961 to 1964.

It was in the middle of 1963 when J.G. Hawkins and family moved from Graham to Romney, Texas, in order to become the pastor of The Church of God, Seventh Day[4]. Bill Hawkins and family would follow him early in 1965, moving to Cross Plains, Texas.

On March 19, 1965, Bill leased property in Cross Plains for one year

---

3   The name of the mother of four of Bill's daughters has been changed to protect the privacy of the innocent and some of their feelings.

4   The Church of God, Seventh Day, in Romney is now the Assembly of Yahweh, 7th Day, Romney, Texas, PO Box 509, Cisco, TX 76437. www.halleluyah.org. Their roots are not in The House of Yahweh and they had no religious affiliation with Buffalo Bill Hawkins when he was living in Cross Plains and Rising Star, Texas. See Appendix Two.

for the purpose of a used car lot. Bill also bought coin operated laundry businesses in Cross Plains and Rising Star. The money for these business ventures came from the sale of part of Dena's inheritance, her Tribal Indian Lands in Oklahoma.

During this period Bill also sold stainless steel cookware, set up a welding shop in the back of his house, and started running and raising coon hounds for sale.

In 1967, Bill sold his unsuccessful business ventures in Cross Plains and Rising Star and moved to Abilene, Texas, with his family and coon dogs. This move was not only prompted by the fact that Bill's businesses had failed, there was also an incident told about him being caught red-handed committing adultery with a married woman in that community.

Instead of Bill watching over his business interests in Cross Plains and Rising Star, he performed as a wrestler for a while, drove around as a passenger in the local police car, and became interested in law enforcement and other exciting adventures.

When Bill and family moved to Abilene, Texas, he was accepted by the police department and graduated from the Abilene Police Academy as a rookie on June 26, 1967. He obtained his Basic Certificate on December 20, 1968, from the Texas Commission on Law Enforcement Officer Standards and Education. Bill remained a Basic Patrolman for the entire nine years of his commission.

Bill and Dena would have their fourth daughter while living in Abilene, and Dena would also start working as a nurse to earn her own money. During this time, Bill took out personal loans without Dena's knowledge, bought two old, very small, trailer houses, and moved them to Lake Fort Phantom Hill just outside of Abilene. He rented one to a friend of his, and he moved his new girlfriend into the other one, a woman I knew, who worked on the same line that I did at Timex Corporation.

From the time that Buffalo Bill Hawkins was born in 1934 until the year 1967 when he joined the police department, he had held numerous jobs, but could not remain employed, and he started numerous businesses, which ultimately failed. He also had numerous affairs with numerous women—and nothing that happened during this entire span of time, to hear him tell it, was ever, never, any of his fault.

Our Beginning Together

Saturday morning, December 16, 1972, I met Bill Hawkins for the second time. While he helped me remove my mobile home tires from the trunk of my car and helped me stack them in the corner of the building, he turned on the charm and flashed a grin from ear to ear. I was assured by Bill Hawkins that he was "not married," that he "ran" Ready Trailer Park where I lived, and that he "ran" a hunting dog kennel, that he "owned" a house in Abilene, and that he was employed as a patrolman on the Abilene Police Department. "So this was the reason that the police car came through the park so often," I thought to myself.

I also found that he was attracted to me. Here was a man, I was thinking, who had ambition and perseverance, and who was on his way to wealth if he was not already there. He held down a full time job and lived in a real house. A heady combination of the exact traits I was looking for in a man, and here he was, established and fourteen years older than me—roots and security.

My third profound religious experience occurred on the day that Bill first invited me to visit him in his home. During the course of our conversation I clearly remember Bill saying, "Do you know that you don't go to heaven when you die?" I remember saying, "I have always believed that." My own religious beliefs were validated at that moment. It was as if a lightning bolt had jolted me into a spiritual awakening. I would never be the same again.

Bill asked me for a date for that following Saturday night and I accepted. Bill tried his best to impress me and was making a fairly positive impression.

However, that impression became quite tarnished that same night. I learned that it was Bill who was the one who fathered the baby daughter with the woman I had worked with at Timex. She was pregnant at the same time that I was pregnant with David, only she gave birth to a daughter a little before I went on maternity leave. Gossip about her and her affair with a police officer flourished. No woman during this era could be pregnant and unmarried without being marked and stigmatized.

When I learned that night that Bill was the Abilene Police Officer who had fathered her daughter, my estimation of Buffalo Bill Hawkins sank like a rock. Bill got out of the car to buy me a soda at a convenience store and left me sitting there, stunned. As I sat there, I began thinking: "What had I gotten into? This man is nothing but a dog. Do I really want to have anything to do with him?"

I then began to think of my past experiences with men. What had I received from them? I began to think of my three beautiful children whom I dearly loved, and the realization that I wanted them to be better off than they were now. A man could change; Buffalo Bill Hawkins could change. I could take this redneck hick cowboy with his peeled haircut and weak chin, and make something of out of him and of me. There was definitely potential.

I found someone who could give me the security I wanted for myself and my children, and who seemed to have the keys to the religion that I had been looking for since childhood. I thought I had found everything that I had been searching for. I chose to overlook the obvious. I settled for Buffalo Bill Hawkins, for better or for worse.

CHAPTER TWO

1973-1974
Business Partners, 50-50

Just after January 1, 1973, Timex called me to come back to work. I told Bill about the phone call, but he did not want me to go back. Intuitively, I knew in order to remain with Bill that I would have to do as he wanted. So, I did not go back to work for Timex. I went to work for Bill Hawkins and myself. I began keeping the business books of Ready Trailer Park, and I saw there was potential for profit.

Bill and I had a relationship with each other, an arrangement by which two people negotiate with each other for a better life together. Equal Partners was its basis, a relationship attested by the fact that our 1973 Business Income Tax Return for Ready Trailer Park showed us to be equal owners: 50-50.

I was still living in my mobile home as this was taking place, and by the end of February I found that I was pregnant.

My divorce from Teddy became final in March of 1973. I moved in with Buffalo Bill Hawkins in April, without the benefit of a legal marriage certificate.

As part of my business duties, it was my job to write out the checks for the monthly bills. I found I was regularly making monthly payments to Singer Corporation, Montgomery Ward, Lerner Shops, Whites Auto Stores, JC Penney, and Sears, but I did not find any "new stuff" in Bill's house to justify the payments. When I asked Bill about this, he told me that he was paying off his ex-wife's things, saying that Dena had charged items to their accounts when she left him. This seemed quite logical. I simply thought that Dena and her children had some new things when they left, and that it was appropriate that Bill should pay for them.

This is what I was allowed to believe at the time, only to find out later in life there was a much different story. DeeDee and I were visiting with Bill's daughters in the fall of 1995. One of Bill's older daughters told us that Bill would tell their mother that he was going hunting, and would load up his coon-dogs in his truck and leave the house, but would not allow Dena's oldest child, her son, to go with him. This was not normal, because he had always gone with Bill before. So when Bill left one evening, he followed him.

He saw Bill drive out to Lake Fort Phantom Hill and enter a small trailer house parked near the lake. He drove back home and told Dena what he had seen. Mother and son drove back to the lake. They opened the door to the trailer and caught Bill and the "other woman," red-handed in bed. Dena determined to leave Bill that night.

The next day Dena put her children in her station wagon, and made purchases at Singer Store (a new sewing machine), Montgomery Ward, Lerner Shop, JC Penney, and Sears (new clothes for everyone and toys for the children), and White's Auto. Dena rented a moving trailer, had everything packed, and was ready to drive away.

Bill had been stalking them, waiting. As soon as they were ready to leave, Bill drove up in his patrol car and blocked their way. He began pulling everything out of the trailer in a fit of rage and burned all their new purchases. He also pulled her new baby doll out of her arms, the first new toy that she ever had, and threw it into the fire. Dena and her children left Abilene with the clothes on their backs, their luggage in the trunk of the car, and some money that Dena had earned while being employed as a nurse.

Knowing what I know now about this story, I now know why Bill did the things that he did. Although I was doing my best to make our relationship work, he exerted physical and mental abuse against me and against my children. The first time Bill hit me in the face was just after I had moved into his house.

Dennis was in the back yard, a small child of age 6, and he had not completed a task to Bill's specifications. Bill was insanely screaming at him. I went outside and told Bill to stop. Bill turned around, doubled up his right fist, and hit me between the eyes.

Why didn't I leave him then? A simple question for a complex situation. Remember, I had been a two-time loser in the marriage game and was determined that this would not be number three. I knew that we were equal partners in a growing business, but I quickly learned that Bill certainly was not worth much at that moment. Any property that was paid for was in his name. We weren't married, so I couldn't get the house. We had entered a business partnership, but the valuable property was mortgaged. All I could expect to get if I had left Bill in April of 1973, was a few hundred dollars for the titles to a few, ratty, old trailer houses, and "maybe" $50.00 a month child support for the child I was carrying at the time; that is, if I was able to hire an attorney. Oh, did I mention that Bill had paid off my mobile home which had been collateral on Teddy's loan, so I didn't even own my mobile home anymore? Did I say that Bill was also making monthly payments to the bank on my car, which had also been collateral for the loan that Teddy had taken out, so I didn't really own my car? He was also paying off my divorce decree expenses and payments on my dishwasher. These reasons for staying were significant since I had no other place to go but home to my parents, and if I went, I would be empty handed.

Bill came to his senses and broke down into a blithering cry-baby. So apologetic, "this will never happen again," he "vowed." In his frenzy of "emotional pain," he smashed the bathroom lavatory with his fist and had to replace it the next day. I was promptly presented an expensive bouquet of roses. Through the years I acquired many vases. I could see the writing on this wall. There was something wrong with this man; he did not have normal emotions because he was not normal. I had to watch out for us.

I decided to stay, drama included. I had a huge goose egg on my forehead, which digressed into two huge black eyes. Around that same time I had accidentally backed my car into an electric pole at the trailer park. There was a huge crater in the bumper and trunk. I told my parents that I hit my forehead when I backed into the pole. I think they wanted to believe me.

To this day Bill does not understand what he forfeited the moment he hit me. The bible says that he who sows the wind will reap the whirlwind. I never trusted Bill from that moment on. I was always on guard, vigilant to preserve the interests of myself and my children regardless of the circumstances. I always remembered his behavior.

To finalize my utter dependence upon him, Bill gave away my car. I later learned that Dena's son had called Bill and told him he needed a car. Bill told him he had a car for him. One day the young man showed up on our doorstep and identified himself. I invited him into the house. I called Bill at work; he came home almost immediately. I was surprised that my car was leaving, even though it was caved in at the back. I thought we would get it repaired. Bill did not discuss this transaction with me first. I signed over the title, and Bill handed him the title and the keys.

He only learned about the condition of the car when he saw it for the first time. The lid to the trunk would not close, so it was partially secured with a flexible rubber cord. Every time the car hit a bump the trunk lid would bounce up and down. When he drove off I could see his humiliation. I was grieved to see that he was being treated badly and that my car, the only thing I had still owned, was leaving. I remember that Bill had a smirk on his face.

By June of 1973, the Partnership: Bill Hawkins and Phyllis Daniel, Ready Trailer Park Rental, 1350 South Treadaway, Abilene, Texas 79602, owned 19 rental trailers.

At the end of June, 1973, Bill took Dennis and me fishing with him at Toledo Bend Reservoir in East Texas. Our first vacation was a fiasco. I felt like a prisoner being forced against her will to do something. I never had a moment of privacy or rest. I was four and one-half months pregnant with Margo, and all I was doing was sitting in a boat, fishing and sun-burning, on a hot, sultry lake during the day, and cooking and cleaning at night.

On our return from this trip, there was an incident which steeled me to leave Bill Hawkins, but it turned out differently. Bill, Dennis, and I drove in from Toledo Bend and the next day, a Sunday, we drove to my parent's home in Royston, Texas, to get DeeDee and David. The children loved visiting their grandparents; it was a complete change from the relentless discipline administered in the house on Poplar Street.

When we returned home late that Sunday afternoon, David became fussy. It was hot and sultry in the house. He was only about 8-months-old, and unable to communicate pain or discomfort except by crying. Bill declared that David had been spoiled by my mother who held him too much. Bill took David from my arms, and carried him to the children's room where he laid David on the bottom bunk, crying. Bill came out of the room and we started arguing about this. During the course of the argument, David stopped crying. Bill said, "See, I told you he would settle down." I walked back into the kitchen and Bill sat down on the couch to watch television. Suddenly, a sense of disaster came over me. I walked right past Bill Hawkins sitting on the couch, right into the children's room, and found David, wedged between the wall and the bed with his face buried in the mattress. I screamed, pulled him out of the bed, and ran to the living room carrying his limp body. Bill jerked him from me and administered infant CPR, blowing two breaths into David's lungs. I was crying hysterically, praying to the Heavenly Father to save David, and feeling sick with guilt that I had killed one of my mother's beloved grandchildren.

Bill stopped administering CPR and laid David on the couch. Bill gave up on David. He came over to where I was kneeled, and began gibbering that David was innocent, that he would rise again, and that I should have hope in the resurrection. My immediate reaction was that Bill Hawkins was nothing but a rotten stench to me and that I was leaving as soon as I could contact my mother. I screamed, "NOOOO!" At almost that same moment David gasped for air and started crying. I ran over to him, grabbed him up, and demanded that we go to the emergency room immediately.

We left Dennis, age 6, in charge of DeeDee, age 2 ½, while we drove to Hendrick Hospital. I remember my conversation with Bill Hawkins on the way. I told Bill that he was crazy and cruel, and that I would never again do something like that to one of my children, and that he wouldn't either. I also remember thinking at the time that Bill better be glad that David was alive, because I would have left him immediately without looking back even once. I also would have brought legal charges against him which would have effectively ended his career in disgrace with the Abilene Police Department.

In July, 1973, Bill and I drove to Oklahoma to get his daughters and bring them back to Abilene for the remainder of the summer. Their ages at the time were 12, 11, 9, and 5. My son, Dennis, was 6, DeeDee was

2 ¾, and David was 9-months-old. I was twenty-five-years old and by then about five months' pregnant with Margo Eileen Hawkins. I had seven children to care for, besides being exhausted cleaning on the rent trailers, cooking three meals a day, and trying to keep my own house clean. I was cranky and tired. I also had no help from Bill Hawkins. In his generation "real men" did not do housework. Bill did, however, bark orders to the children to "do this" and "do that," which was very endearing of him while he sat on his butt on the couch.

Another wonderful idea Bill had in the middle of July was to go on another camping trip with everyone but DeeDee and David. They stayed with my parents. I do not even remember where we went, only that I continued to cook three meals a day and never had a private moment to myself. Bill also expected instant obedience from any child around him, and expected to be the center of attention at all times. A child would not be allowed to have many of his or her emotional needs met. There seemed to be a rivalry between him and his children. I could not understand this, so I could not effectively deal with it. At a time when the children should have been enjoying themselves and having great fun, they were restricted and excessively disciplined. When Bill wanted to do something, everybody had to do it. Neither they nor I had very much fun.

Afterward, the situation at home grew worse. The girls finally got fed up and tried to take their frustration out on me. I remember the time they got together in their room one evening while Bill was on patrol, and began chanting part of the theme song from *The Addam's Family,* a popular television program at the time: Da-da-da-DUM! (fingers snapped twice) da-da-da-DUM! (snap, snap) da-da-da-DUM, da-da-da-DUM, da-da-da-DUM (snap, snap). This was repeated, over and over.

Looking back, it was hilarious. At the time it was happening, it was anarchy. Bill had somehow gotten it into his head that we would all be this one, big, happy family, and that Bill would just keep his girls with him. The problem was these girls had a mother and brother back home, and they were homesick.

The other problem Bill's daughters had with me would not be known until years later. I found out that they were of the opinion that it was "me" who was caught red-handed with Bill in the trailer house on

Lake Fort Phantom Hill. They thought that I was the "snake" who had broken up their family. It would not be until 1993 that Bill's youngest daughter told her sisters that I was not the "evil woman" who had done the deed. For twenty years I was blamed for something that Bill and his "other woman" had done to his family in 1972.

When the date came nearer that the girls would go home to their mother in Oklahoma, I took them on a shopping trip to buy a few new clothes for school. I am looking at a check stub where I noted that I spent $26.00 at K-Mart for one of the girls. Bill complained that I had spent too much money, and that I would not be allowed to take them shopping again. Bill had to have absolute control and all the praise. If he spent the money, it would have been just fine. That summer was the first and last time all the girls came together to visit their dad.

November 8, 1973, started out to be a normal day. I was in a full term pregnancy, but cleaned two trailers, prepared an evening meal including dessert, had dined, and had cleaned the table and kitchen. I had bathed and dressed Dennis, DeeDee, and David, and then went into hard labor. Margo Eileen Hawkins, a beautiful baby girl, was born on push number three. I spent two nights in the hospital and came home. I rested one week, and was then back to my normal routine—business as usual growing the business of our Partnership, 50-50—acquiring more mobile homes to acquire more income.

December 25, 1973, is the first time that my children and I did not keep Christmas. I remember missing my family so much during this time, and I know my family missed my children and me. Bill would not allow us to go visit them, and would not even buy our children some toys to play with. I felt miserable, depressed, and alone.

1974

The year, 1974, is written in the bank check stubs which I saved, and gives a snapshot of the life I lived with Bill Hawkins. On January 28, 1974, I celebrated my twenty-sixth birthday. I remember nothing about it except for the fact that I received flowers, since I wrote the check as payment when the bill came in.

In April I made the first payment on the piano that I had wanted. The new Whitney was moved into my living room. I had been out of practice for so long, but wanted the piano. I had taken music lessons. Bill had been a singer with the Whippoorwills, the name of his rock band. At the time I thought music might be an interest we could share. I had no way of knowing at the time that buying this piano would play a pivotal role in our lives in 1976, two years later.

Mr. Otis Hawkins, Bill's dad, passed away on September 6, 1974, from advanced prostate cancer. He had been staying with his daughter and son-in-law in Arlington, Texas. They said Mr. Hawkins went into a coma-like state and became pain free for the first time in months. Mr. Hawkins is buried outside of Graham, Texas, in Tonk Valley Cemetery, next to his wife, Maggie Mae and their son, Vernon George.

The Hawkins family gathered together at Gene's home in Graham to prepare for the funeral. Bill drank like a fish to get through it. At that time I was almost three months pregnant with our son, Justin Bill Hawkins.

Although Mr. Hawkins was laid to rest, the drama was far from over. About a week after the funeral, Bill parked Mr. Hawkins' old pickup on the street in front of our house. When I asked him about the pickup, Bill told me that Mr. Hawkins had given it to him.

I later learned from the family that Bill drove to Graham, got the pickup, and loaded up all of Mr. Hawkins' hogs; while Mr. Hawkins' current wife and children watched him, helplessly. Bill sold the hogs at the local farm auction, pocketed all the money, then drove the pickup back to Abilene.

Bill got the pickup and all the hog money, without sharing with his family. Because of this, his family thought it appropriate that Bill should pay for Mr. Hawkins' funeral balance and land taxes. I wrote a check once a month to the funeral home in Graham until the balance was paid in full.

Immediately after this, Bill set out in a concerted effort to "adopt" Johnny Hawkins, Mr. Hawkins 5-year-old son. All I saw was that Bill wanted to adopt Johnny's Social Security check. We drove to Graham and spoke with local social workers about him. Gratefully, in the end Johnny's mother packed up all her children and left by bus headed east; where, I do not know. I never heard from Johnny again, and if Bill heard from him he didn't tell me. By the check stub, it was in November of

1974 that we paid our attorney for the consultation concerning this sordid "adoption" business.

The bible says that those who seek for gold will never be satisfied with gold. This was my exasperation and frustration in 1974. Bill and I were building a successful business. We had a new car and were accumulating "good stuff," but I was not satisfied. Bill and I had been writing checks to J.G. Hawkins for tithes. Occasionally we would receive booklets from Jacob entitled, *The Prophetic Watchman*. From Jacob Hawkins' writings, he proclaimed that he was the Watchman to warn the wicked and the righteous of things yet to come. *The Plain Truth*, a publication of The Worldwide Church of God founded by Herbert W. Armstrong, was also being sent to our home on a monthly basis, but we had yet to send any money to this organization.

The writings in these two magazines stirred me spiritually and were relevant to my religious education. I desired to have fellowship with those of like mind but, in 1974, Bill did not share this interest. It was while Bill was in Cox Hospital recovering from his appendectomy, in June, 1974, that I promised that I would also tithe to The Worldwide Church of God.

I wrote a check to this organization, but Bill ranted when he learned how much. Bill finally agreed to pay, but he determined the amounts. I continued paying tithes, receiving literature, and growing in interest in the Law, Sabbaths, and Sacred Name Teachings.

In December of 1974 there are only notations for mobile home payments, bills, and expenses. However, there were no holidays to celebrate. We did not keep Christmas. We did not celebrate the Jewish Chanukkah. We did not visit relatives during December because my parents might get my children some toys.

However, Bill set off to Colorado on a deer hunt and was gone for several days, leaving me and the children alone. When he arrived back at the house, I had dinner prepared. Margo was just a little over 13-months-old and started to cry about something as she sat in her highchair. I couldn't believe my eyes when I saw Bill slap her on her leg. She was startled, then she was terrified. Bill got in one more slap before I could stop it. The fight was on. Bill finally got what he wanted when he came into the house—to be the center of attention regardless of how he got it.

There was also a gaping spiritual void, and eventually every vacuum gets filled. Here we were, paying tithes to The Worldwide Church of God and to J.G. Hawkins, but I did not know a soul from these organizations. I was grieving for my family and some fellowship that December of 1974. Bill and I had more than one conversation about contacting The Worldwide Church of God throughout 1974, but nothing came of the conversations. Bill was also working on Saturdays and seemed to be content with this.

Another fact, I soon came to understand, was that The Worldwide Church of God was a very exclusive organization. If one was married, one had to be living with one's first and only husband or wife, or one had to be in a single state if one was divorced. There was no room for sinners in this organization.

Then, the floodgate opened when Mr. Herbert W. Armstrong declared that divorce was no longer a cardinal sin. There was no longer a stigma, so divorced people were now welcome in The Worldwide Church of God. My time had come.

CHAPTER THREE

1975-1976
Life with Religion

Early in the month of January, 1975, I was informed that Jacob Hawkins and his family would be returning to the United States. Jacob wrote about his move in *The Prophetic Watchman,* in an article entitled, "From Nazareth to Odessa." He did not write in his magazine that he and his family stopped at our house in Abilene first.

I remember Jacob as a gray-haired man with a gray beard. He wore a black hat, slacks, and tie, with a white shirt. At the time Jacob would have been fifty years-of-age, ten years older than Bill. I remember that Isabel, who was forty-five at the time, wore a white pants-suit and a green blouse, which set off her lovely, long red hair very becomingly. Jacob's two sons were teenagers. I remember them having small goatee beards, looking like somber hippies. Jacob's daughter had long brown hair, and was slender and pretty. Her fiancée had accompanied them. It was necessary that he report to the U.S. Immigration Office in San Antonio, Texas, to register and begin the process of becoming a United States citizen. This project would be more convenient to accomplish from Abilene, Texas, rather than from Odessa.

Almost as soon as they arrived, Jacob, Isabel, daughter, and future son-in-law got into a car belonging to a woman who I had previously met, and they left for San Antonio. I then offered food to the two young men, fed my children, and laid down to rest, since I was around eight-months-pregnant.

At some point that evening everyone returned. It was then that I noticed Isabel's behavior. She seemed nervous, agitated, and anxious about something. Tension seemed to race through the air. Jacob did not help the situation. He snapped angrily, and told Isabel to settle down and be quiet.

I remember meeting this woman for the first time around October, 1974. She and Ruby Maynard dropped by our house on their way to the Jewish synagogue in Abilene to attend services on the Day of Atonement. Bill was on patrol for the police department, and they were surprised that he was not at home. She was a lovely woman, well-groomed, with perfectly curled, medium length, brown hair, pretty jewelry, and a warm smile. It would be several years later before I learned the bitter circumstances which caused the tension on that day.[5]

Bill took Jacob to see our land at 1025 T&P Lane in Abilene after their return. We had acquired ten and one-half acres earlier, in 1974, in order to expand our mobile home park business. When we learned that Jacob was returning to the States, we decided to offer Jacob the use of this land in order to build the organization, The House of Yahweh. Bill also offered to help Jacob become established in Abilene. Jacob wanted nothing to do with either offer.

Here I was, still without the fellowship of another spiritual woman close by. But I was determined to make the best of the situation—I would go to Odessa to observe Yahweh's Feasts. The next day Jacob, Isabel, and children drove on to Odessa, Texas. Although disappointed, on reflection there were probably two reasons that Jacob did not want to remain in Abilene—to be as far away as he could get from Buffalo Bill Hawkins, and also from this same woman.

On January 28, 1975, Bill organized a surprise birthday party for me. The problem was that Bill was absolutely hateful to me that whole morning. I was very depressed when the guests began to arrive that afternoon, among them Mother, Daddy, and Mr. and Mrs. Daugherty. Bill brought in the surprise cake and flowers. Bill then turned on the charm for the enjoyment of our guests and I guess that he expected me to follow suit. Bill probably meant well, but the best gift he could have given me was never offered: peace, harmony, and respect. Bill also wanted to make sure that I knew exactly how much he had spent on a

---

5   See Appendix Two

ring that he had bought me for the occasion; I wrote the check when the statement was sent to the house.

It was on February 23, 1975, that I told Bill I was going to call my mother and ask her to come to our home the next day to stay with Dennis, DeeDee, David, and Margo when I went into the hospital to have our baby. The question was asked, "How do you know?" I just knew. Mother came the next afternoon. Around 5:00 in the morning on February 25, 1975, I woke up with strong labor contractions.

Primal screams sounded from my chest, which Bill could hear as he stood at the entrance to the delivery suite. Justin Bill Hawkins was delivered, the only son born to Buffalo Bill Hawkins. Bill was elated. He only had daughters previously, six that I knew of to this point. I actually deceived myself into thinking that our relationship would be better, since Bill had the son that he always wanted.

Justin was circumcised on his eighth day of life according to the scriptures. I believe that it was Justin's circumcision and Jacob's teachings which caused Bill to start thinking about his own state of being uncircumcised.

Bill was also thinking about his real name. He was embarrassed about it, and I was embarrassed for him. In March, 1975, I ordered a copy of Bill's Birth Certificate from the State of Oklahoma. "Buffalo Bill Hawkins" was named after the cowboy movie star, Buffalo Bill Cody. Bill attempted to change his name by simply writing it on the certificate, but that was denied. He had to legally change his name if he wanted to be named Justin Bill Hawkins, the name we had given our son.

We were invited to Jacob's daughter's wedding in the middle of March. This ceremony was performed in a Jewish Temple in Odessa— under the canopy in the Jewish tradition. The men in the congregation wore tallits and kippahs; it was so exotic. The local Rabbi performed the ceremony. The groom smashed the wineglass into slivers with the heel of his shoe, and we attended a small reception in Jacob and Isabel's home afterward.

The Feast of Passover and Unleavened Bread was set for March 27 through April 2, 1975. Jacob set the Passover Seder for Tuesday night, March 25th, and invited us to attend. This Passover Seder was a combination of the Jewish Seder with the Last Supper, Jewish and

Christian observances combined. Bill had to work that day. We left for Odessa about 4:00 in the afternoon.

The Seder was already in progress when we entered Jacob's house, late for the appointment. We were seated around Jacob's kitchen table, next to Jacob and his family and Tex and his family. I had already met Tex and family when they had returned from Israel in 1974.

This was the very first Seder I had ever attended. I saw tiny glasses of wine passed around to drink. I saw crackers being dipped into something and eaten, then hardboiled eggs followed. I didn't understand the ceremony or its meaning. I tried to listen carefully to what Jacob was reading. I wondered where each of these traditions was written about in the bible. I thought to myself, "I'm really ignorant of the scriptures so what do I know." Later Bill told me that I had made Jacob uncomfortable by staring at him.

We returned to Abilene that night. Bill had to go to work the next day. We did not eat any leavened bread for the full week in observance of the Feast of Unleavened Bread.

Bill's shoulder and ribs became excruciatingly painful in June. Bill just knew he had a terminal cancer and became very depressed that he might die just as he had a son born to him. He finally went to a physician and the diagnosis was Gout. Bill was prescribed a drug, and was told to take it for the rest of his life to prevent further gout attacks.

It was during the summer of 1975, that Bill finally relented and scheduled our first tentative meeting with a representative of The Worldwide Church of God. I wondered if they would be as strange as Jacob, although the people pictured in their magazines looked normal. The Worldwide Church of God minister, who was pastor of the churches in Midland, San Angelo, and Abilene, was Charles (Chuck) Dickerson. He and his beautiful wife came to our house for our first interview.

Bill coached me to tell them that my first husband had died in a fatal auto accident, which was true, and he coached me not to mention that I had a second, divorced, husband who was still living at the time. He also told me to say that I was married to him. All of this word-play just to attend church. During the course of our interview, Chuck noted that I had a piano in the living room and asked if I played. I told him that I was out of practice.

We were invited to attend services with The Worldwide Church of

God, but we did not immediately do so. There would be another power play with lots of drama. I wanted to buy myself and my children some new clothes in which to go to church. Bill said we couldn't afford it. I interpreted Bill's meaning to be: "I really don't want to go." Well, I wanted to go, and I wanted new clothes to go in. I proceeded to inform Bill that if he could afford a boat, equity in rent mobile homes, and all of his hunting expenses, why couldn't I afford new clothes for me and my children? After the fight, I paid by check for the flowers. We would not attend services with The Worldwide Church of God until late that fall.

We visited Jacob and his family on a fairly regular basis during the summer of 1975, so I had fellowship with them. But some of their traditions were very strange to me. The men wore a hat or a kippah at all times; the women wore a head covering. Women should wear their hair long, but keep it covered so not much of it could be seen. Jacob also taught that one must not eat milk and meat together at the same meal.

The more we visited with Jacob, the more Bill felt compelled to be circumcised, and not only him, but Dennis (age 8) and David (age 22 months) would also become circumcised.

Mother came to stay with DeeDee, Margo, and Justin as she questioned my sanity.

Check-in time at Hendrick Hospital was after 5:00 pm the day before. Bill was in the Surgical Wing and Dennis and David were in the Pediatric Ward. I tried to be at two different places in the same hospital at the same time. The surgeries were performed in August, 1975, by Dr. Paul Mani. Dennis and David were scheduled the first thing the next morning, with the benefit of anesthesia. Bill went into surgery after that, without anesthesia. Bill said that he remembered everything.

What I remember is him having stitches where the foreskin was cut away, him experiencing excruciating pain on a regular basis, and him being in a constant state of anger until his surgical wound was healed. Finally, all the men in my household were circumcised.

This year we planned to keep the first two days and last day of the Feast of Tabernacles with The House of Yahweh in Odessa, Texas. As the feast season approached, the month of September was spent shopping and preparing. We called and reserved a motel room close to The House of Yahweh in Odessa, Texas.

The Feast of Trumpets and Day of Atonement were observed, then the Feast of Tabernacles was close at hand. Bill scheduled off work on Friday, September 19. We drove to Odessa and checked into our motel room. The next day was the High Day, so we dressed and attended services at 10:00 in the morning. We stayed for lunch, visited in the afternoon, stayed for dinner, visited, and went back to our motel room. Late the following Sunday afternoon, we drove back to Abilene so Bill could go to work on Monday.

The next Saturday, September 27, was the Last Great Day of the feast, so we again drove to Odessa and attended services.

I think we would have eventually joined The House of Yahweh in Odessa— if I had not experienced this feast in the specific way that I did. I can remember there were not many people. I also remember that immediately after each service the women dutifully marched to the kitchen to cook every meal, while the men retired to a private conference room to sit and talk. I also felt the majority of the sermons were empty and void of spiritual benefit. I went to learn, but instead I endured one boring, dry sermon after another, with each speaker seeming to contradict the other one.

Some, but not all, of the women wore long skirts, long sleeved blouses, no makeup, with their hair tied under a headscarf. I would never become one of those strange, defeated women. That experience was enough for me. I was determined to attend The Worldwide Church of God. When we got home I was on the phone trying to contact someone from that organization.

On October 4, 1975, the first Saturday after the Feast of Tabernacles, my children and I attended our first Sabbath services with The Worldwide Church of God in Abilene, Texas. I had decided that I was going whether Bill went or not. He was on patrol for the Abilene Police Department that Saturday, as usual.

As my children and I were getting into the car to attend the 2:00 afternoon service, one of Bill's hunting buddies drove up behind me in the driveway. He got out of his pickup, walked to the car, and asked me to get the registration papers for one of Bill's champion hunting dogs. He said he wanted to enter the dog in some sort of competition. I told him that I would not be able to get the papers, since I was already leaving. I told him that Bill could get them for him. He told me that Bill had told him that I would give him these papers. I said I was sorry about that.

Nothing was going to stop me. I backed around his truck and drove to the afternoon service of The Worldwide Church of God, Abilene congregation. My children and I, wearing our new clothes, were very warmly welcomed. I was among friends and peers the moment I walked in.

I remember the sermon was about the Feast of Tabernacles, how wonderful it had been, and the necessity of returning to a normal life after experiencing such a heavenly event. I was in heaven, spiritually, just being there. This description of the Feast of Tabernacles celebrated by The Worldwide Church of God was quite different than that which I had just experienced at The House of Yahweh in Odessa.

I remember meeting a wonderful woman that first Sabbath. I had been reading the publications of The Worldwide Church of God for quite a while. I was well versed in Armstrong's teachings. The more we spoke, the more she was determined that I was ready for baptism, and, at her urging, I approached Chuck Dickerson about this subject.

I had enough understanding to know that one does not profess to be ready for baptism one week and the next week the event is scheduled. In The Worldwide Church of God it took many weeks of study to become a baptized member; but I wanted to start the process.

Later that night I mentioned to Bill that I had discussed baptism with Chuck Dickerson. The way Bill reacted to this might have led someone to believe that I had committed adultery with him instead. Out of the blue, Bill angrily accused me of "usurping authority" over him; that if his wife wanted baptism it should have been him that asked, not her. I proceeded to inform Bill that it would have been rather hard for him to ask the pastor about anything, since he was riding around in a patrol car, working on the Sabbath Day. All hell broke loose and we were fighting it out, this time Bill just hitting me on the top of my head and on my back, where the bruises would not show.

Of course, I lost. Flowers arrived the next day with the same contrite "vow" that Bill always broke: "This will never happen again."

Every Sabbath Day after this my children and I went to services, without him. I believe it was his embarrassment about the situation that finally forced Bill to act; he took steps to request to be scheduled off from work, so he could go with me.

One day during the first week of November, 1975, there was a confrontation between Bill Hawkins and the Chief of Police, Warren Dodson, about this request. I do not know what words were spoken by Bill when he made it. He had eight years' seniority on the job at the time. I only know the result: Bill began to take off work from Friday at sunset through Saturday at sunset.

Bill finally started attending services with The Worldwide Church of God, Abilene, on Saturday, November 8, 1975. At first, Bill wore his leisure suits without a tie. The other men wore suits and ties. Bill sat and read his bible as the congregation stood and sang. When the preaching service began, Bill began reading something else, and tried to distract me from listening to the sermon by trying to talk to me. I came to the point that I wished Bill would just stay at home if he didn't want to be here.

We also went on with our own business and pleasure. Bill had gotten a license for a CB Radio, which he used on his deer hunting trips. We enrolled DeeDee in ballet class. We closed on our property in Eula, Texas, for 35.98 acres of land, upon which I lived until 2006.

When we first acquired this property together in 1975, the only building on the land was a cowshed at the north property line. The only improvements were a pond, a water well, and an iron gate. The first building we constructed was a large shop with a cement floor and sheet metal walls and roof.

On December 31, 1975, a beautiful, warm winter day, Bill and I, with our younger children, drove to a nursery to buy pecan trees, fig trees, grape vines, and peach trees.

The next day, January 1, 1976, a "blue norther" came in, but we left our warm home in Abilene and drove out to Eula. We were freezing as we tried to plant some of those trees. Dennis, a little 9-year-old boy, was working with a hired man, digging holes; cold, hard, miserable work. The only shelter we had was a little camping trailer and the new shop. Shivering, Bill and I went in the trailer where the younger children were placed; Dennis and the other man did not. I then threw a tantrum and demanded that they be allowed to stop. I bundled Dennis up in the truck as we drove back to Abilene.

We eventually planted those 40 pecan trees. Some of them survived, and are now large beautiful trees which I could see from my kitchen window.

This is the year that we built up our farm and it took most of our time. Dennis went to school all day in Abilene, but DeeDee only went half a day for kindergarten, which began 12:00 noon. When they got out of school they were required to walk straight home, about four blocks, and remain in the back yard until we returned from working at the farm, usually around 6:00 in the evening.

Bill began the process of legally adopting our three oldest children at the end of April. He said that everyone should have the same last name. I know that my children were conflicted about this. They wanted to be a part of the Hawkins family, but I think they wanted to keep their own last names. A social worker was sent to our house in Abilene to interview us and the children. He took each of the children to a separate room and asked them if they wanted to be adopted and change their last name to Hawkins; each said yes. Later, I would learn from DeeDee that this was one of the worst days of her life. Bill had spoken to them behind my back, and they had been pressured by him to agree.

On Saturday, April 4, 1976, I became a baptized member of The Worldwide Church of God. Elder Charles Dickerson presided.

This is the year that Bill became the Song Leader for the congregation, and this is how he obtained this position.

The first time I had attended church with The Worldwide Church of God, I noted there was a pianist. The next Saturday there was no pianist. Sometime later there was another pianist but she could not continue for some reason. The local leaders of the Abilene congregation were a Deacon and his wife. Their son, a graduate of the highly esteemed Ambassador College in Pasadena, California, was the song leader.

One Sunday afternoon Chuck and his wife came to our house while Bill was there, and asked me to be the pianist for the church. Immediately afterward, several things went through my mind. First, I wanted to do this. Second, Bill would abuse me if I played the piano while the other young man led the singing, so eventually I would be forced to quit. Third, I knew Bill could sing, even though he refused to do so during any of the previous services. Fourth, Bill had not been asked to become the song leader.

It was then that I politely told Chuck that I would be glad to be the pianist if Bill could lead the singing. This is how Bill became the Song Leader for The Worldwide Church of God, Abilene.

Bill bought a new suit and tie in order to be appropriately dressed. Both of us practiced daily. An elderly couple in the congregation came to our home and tuned my piano on a regular basis.

Dennis was enrolled in Little League while DeeDee was still going to ballet. Bill drove to Midland and bought the 19-foot-boat in which we would fish during our vacations in Port Aransas, Texas. Our weekdays were filled with work, baseball, and ballet; our weekends were filled with church and visiting my parents. I don't know what I would have done without my mother.

We sent a check to Bill's girls for school clothes. They did not come to visit us this year.

In the middle of all these activities, we continued building up our farm. We were pioneers, back to nature and being self-sufficient; fresh milk and eggs, vegetables picked from the garden, a place of my own, safety and security. My children and I worked as hard as Bill on this farm. I was also an equal partner in this arrangement, 50-50.

On the surface our lives looked perfect. Beneath the surface lurked insecurity and resentment. Bill had insisted that I carry on the charade that I was married to him, which I was not. Each of our children now had his last name but I did not have a marriage certificate, and this is what I wanted.

One thing which prevented Bill from becoming legally married me, was the fact that he was still legally married to Rosa Bell Bolding Hawkins, to whom he was married when he was eighteen-years-old, and from whom he did not get legally divorced. When Bill met Dena, the mother of four of his daughters, he simply began living with her. He never legally married Dena because he said he couldn't. I believed him.

However, I wanted to be a respectable married woman, and many of our conversations focused on this topic.

Bill took steps in 1976 to divorce Rosa Bell Bolding Hawkins. Dan S. Abbott was Bill's legal counsel in Cause 11961 in the Court of Domestic Relations, Taylor County, Texas, in the matter of the Marriage of B.B. Hawkins and Rosa Bell Hawkins. In the Affidavit for Citation by Publication (since Rosa Bell could not be located), Bill stated,

> "I am the Petitioner in the above-captioned and numbered cause. The Respondent in this case, Rosa Bell Hawkins, was last seen by me in approximately the year of 1953, when she left the residence of Respondent and Petitioner. In about the year of 1960, Respondent made a phone call from the State of California to Petitioner's father, not at that time revealing her whereabouts."

Inquiry had been made in every County Clerk's office in all counties of California and Oklahoma, to verify if a divorce action had already taken place. There was no divorce on file in these States.

As the feast season approached, the first part of the month of September was spent preparing for an eight day feast. The Feast of Trumpets and Day of Atonement were observed. On October 8, 1976, we left Abilene right after Bill got off work. We arrived at Gladewater, Texas, in the early hours of the morning, where we stopped and rested in the camper.

Later that morning we drove to the camp grounds at Big Sandy, Texas, and were escorted to a camp row closer to Lake Loma than to the huge auditorium on the Ambassador College Campus.

The morning service started at 10:00. The choir sang so beautifully the First Holy Day Service. Bill said he would like to audition for a choir position since an invitation had been extended during the morning announcements. I told him to go. When Bill finished auditioning, he had a place in the Tenor Section. Throughout the remainder of this feast, I remember Bill hurrying to choir practice immediately after a light lunch, where he would remain for two to four hours.

Every morning we would get up, eat breakfast, and get ready for church. We would walk about eight blocks to the main auditorium. A different Preaching Elder spoke each day. It was wonderful to be a part of the nearly 10,000 members gathered there. Afternoons were for exploring the area and evenings were for entertainment. The most fun thing was to cook out on the campfire and visit with our neighbors. After we dined, we would sit around the campfire talking and enjoying each others' company, while the children played. I felt as though it was a small taste of what the kingdom would be like. I loved these people.

Another special event was the fact that Mr. Herbert W. Armstrong made a personal appearance during this feast. I will never forget the adulation and applause he received, and I remember the look on Bill's face. It was pure admiration, tinged with envy. I remember thinking that I had seen a very important man. We had a seat fairly close to the podium and were able to see him clearly. He tried to suppress the applause, but it continued. An announcement had been made that picture taking with flashes would not be permitted, since this would disturb Mr. Armstrong's vision. To the best of my memory Mr. Armstrong spoke about the "give" kind of religion, as opposed to the "get" kind.

We attended every service and enjoyed every minute. I remember this feast being very spiritual for me, and regretted that it had to end.

We drove back to Abilene to resume our normal routine, only now Bill was a Legally Divorced Man. Judge J. Neil Daniel had pronounced Bill legally divorced on October 13, 1976, on a weekday during the Feast of Tabernacles. It had taken a good bit of time to get to this point, but I would not become legally married to Buffalo Bill Hawkins until August 1, 1977.

I believe that we would have been married sooner, but circumstances beyond our control prevented this from taking place.

During my research for this book, I have come to the theory that from the moment Bill confronted Police Chief Warren Dodson the previous year—those in power at the time in the Abilene Police Department had set out to find a way to remove Officer Bill Hawkins from their ranks. It is my opinion that these entities eventually found a flimsy excuse to pursue. However frivolous, charges were leveled against Bill and steps were doggedly taken to pursue this purpose.

It would have been Thursday, November 17, 1976, that Bill came to the house while he was still on duty, and asked me to help him fill out some papers from the police department. He didn't tell me at the time that these papers were an "official statement" of events that had occurred while Bill was on duty the night of November 15, 1976, and that his commanding officer had given these to him.

I vaguely remember asking him what this was about, and he said that the other night that he had arrested two Mexicans for being drunk in public, and had to carry one of the men, struggling, and place him in the back seat of the patrol car, and that the other man walked to the passenger side of the patrol car and sat down in the front seat. Due to Bill's explanation, this didn't seem that important to me. Bill had filled out many other mundane police reports while he sat on our couch, so this seemed no different from these other times.

I was swamped with housework, childcare, and bookkeeping, and told him to write his own report since he seemed to know what to say.

So, Bill wrote this by himself, stating that he had left the patrol car "exactly as I found it." He turned this in to his shift commander, Capt. E.L. O'Dell, on the same day, November 17.

On November 22, Bill was called into Capt. O'Dell's office where it was insinuated that Bill had lied in the letter that he had written. It was then that Bill found out that the two men whom he had arrested the night of November 15, 1976, had given affidavits that Bill had taken four cans of beer from them. Bill was then required to write a detailed account of the events that had taken place during his 11:00 pm to 7:00 am shift.

Bill came home and basically told me that it was my fault that his report had gotten him in trouble; that if I had written it like he asked, that this would not be happening to him.

This was the first time that Bill told me that this was an "official report," and that there were four cans of beer involved. This was serious and I was worried.

One of the most important things Daddy had instilled in me was the concept of an honorable name. To me, it looked as though Bill's reputation was being destroyed, and by association so was mine. I insisted that we write a letter of explanation to clarify this misunderstanding, which is exactly what I thought it was. I had observed Bill doing some things which were not quite ethical, but he would write his reports to the officials at the police department and then everything was resolved. Surely, I thought, a letter of clarification would bring this same result.

The problem was, I had not read Bill's first report. Bill did not remember what he had originally written, and the powers in control seemed to be looking for a cause. A small part about the "beer in the car" was changed in this letter, which led to Bill being accused of lying on the first official report.

On November 23, 1976, Bill turned in our four-page letter addressed to Assistant Police Chief Dwain Pyburn, which tried to explain about the trash in the car, the radar equipment on the front floor, and why four cans of beer were still left in the patrol car when Bill left his shift. The following excerpts are from a copy of this letter,

On November 22 I was called into Capt. Odell's office. At this time he insinuated that I might have lied to him in the letter I wrote. At this time it came to my attention that the two suspects I had arrested previously had made out affadavits (sic)[6] to the fact that I had taken four cans of beer from them and since there were four cans of beer found in the car <u>and</u> beer mentioned in my letter, facts naturally fell into place and I am convicted…

After leaving the station I started back to the address on Pecan. As I went by the Diamond Doll Club I noticed a car coming out of the alley behind the club, I hit my brakes and pulled in the station driveway at…to check the club and the car. At that time I noticed the beer. It slid forward in the floor. I checked the club and the car leaving the club. I came back, got in my car and reached down, got the beer with my right hand and put it in the back seat. If I had felt any guilt at all concerning the beer that was mentioned, doesn't it seem plausible that I would have explained it away in great and exact detail? I truthfully thought when the beer slid forward on the floorboard of the patrol car when I hit my brakes, that the officer who used the Car #34 before me had merely forgotten to take the evidence out of his car. I thought whoever it was would come back to get it on his next shift. The beer was in my way in the front so I put it out of my way in the back seat. If I had taken those boys beer, which I didn't, I surely would have stated that the beer was left in the car because I forgot to turn it in as evidence at the time they were arrested and I intended to do that just as soon as I got back down to the station. If I were guilty of this there would have been a lot better letter written. I have been with this Department for nearly 10 years.

6   Sic. Latin adverb. The quotation is literally given, though containing an error in spelling or grammar.

My work is, and always had been, the most important thing to me when I get into a patrol car and I would not jeopardize my job over four little cans of beer, or anything else for that matter. I have been a profitable servant to the City of Abilene and an honest cop. When I leave this job I will leave it under honorable circumstances because I don't deserve any less. Respectfully, (signed Bill Hawkins)

Bill then received a written order from Asst. Chief Dwain Pyburn directing him to take a lie detector test on November 26, 1976. I told Bill to take it and get this issue behind us. To me, my yes would have been yes and my no would have been no. To Bill, he was being "persecuted." When I tried to question Bill to learn why it was that he thought he was being persecuted, he became enraged and refused to answer my questions. I remember Bill being constantly agitated, like a pacing, caged, wild animal.

To me, he was acting guilty of something. There was no adamant statement of innocence, which I would have expected to receive. Instead, he turned and lashed out at me for questioning him. Receiving no reassurance of Bill's innocence, I felt overwhelmed with apprehension and fear.

Bill did not appear to take the lie detector test on November 26, as ordered. On November 28, 1976, on a Sunday, Bill came home and told me that he had been indefinitely suspended from the Abilene Police Department. Now, anger, shame, and embarrassment were added to the emotions I was feeling.

Bill was attending The Worldwide Church of God and was the Song Leader, and now this. I also had to face my parents burdened by a man whose best excuse seemed to me to be that he was being "picked on." I tried my best to assume the position of defending Bill to my parents and my church, but my defense rang hollow.

Somehow, the local media was immediately informed. The story of Bill's suspension was broadcast on the local TV stations and made front page news. This was the only news that was being reported. The Abilene Police Department did not release any statements about the case, and Bill Hawkins also remained silent. Speculation was rampant.

This left a "news vacuum" which the media cried to be filled. Reporters would call our home requesting a statement, and Bill refused to speak to them. I was left holding the phone, and had nothing to say to them. I felt humiliation.

I knew what the official charges were, but I would not know the circumstances surrounding Bill's suspension until they became public in January. Bill continued the posture that he was being "persecuted," but I could sense no hint of embarrassment or remorse from him, and he could not explain what had taken place.

I also "felt persecuted" because the news media was hounding me for information. Bill's name was listed in the local phone book, so the reporters had his number. Bill refused to answer the phone when the reporters called. I would be the one who answered, and who stated that we had "no comment."

Immediately after the news was released all our creditors sent their bills, out of billing cycle. I paid them off. Many times I had spoken to Bill about leaving the police department, since our business was growing and we had more than enough to comfortably live on. At the time, I wanted Bill to leave the police department; I just didn't want him to be fired and his reputation ruined.

Bill hired Ed Cockerell as his attorney. In the course of establishing Bill's defense, Bill sat through two other lie detector sessions.

On December 20, 1976, Billy R. Olsen, Director of the Fire and Police Civil Service Commission of the City of Abilene, Texas, sent a Notice of Meeting to be held at 9:00 am on Wednesday, January 5, 1977, in the City Council Room, Room No. 201, City Hall, 555 Walnut Street, Abilene, Texas, to hear the appeal of Police Officer Bill Hawkins concerning his indefinite suspension from the Abilene Police Department.

This announcement launched another barrage of questions from the news media. Again, Bill refused to speak for himself when the reporters called our home. I had enough. We were moving to our farm in Eula to escape the onslaught. Our home was not built yet, so we bought a used mobile home and set it up in front of our fenced garden. A septic system was installed. During the children's Christmas break we moved to Eula, Texas. Since our phone was no longer listed, the calls ceased for the time being.

Chapter Four

1977

Trial, Exoneration, Marriage

The New Year, 1977, began with me enrolling our older children in the Eula School System and dreading the trial scheduled for January 5th. Bill told me that Ed, Bill's attorney, wanted me to sit by him during his trial. I had never spoken one word to Bill's attorney about anything prior to this, and I told Bill there was no way that I was going to do any such thing. My doubt about his innocence would have shone on my face, as well as my deep embarrassment and shame. I didn't want to be responsible for destroying his defense, so the best thing I did was to stay at home.

Trial-Accusations of Lying

The trial was front page news. Excerpts from the Wednesday Evening, January 5, 1977, edition of *The Abilene Reporter News*,[7] written by Ann Flores, Staff Writer, follow:

> Police Officer Bill Hawkins was suspended November 28 for allegedly lying about leaving a patrol car with four cans of

---

7   All articles cited from *The Abilene Reporter News*, are now owned by the E.W. Scripps Company, 312 Walnut Street, Suite 2800, Cincinnati, Ohio 45202, and are used without their objection and with my gratitude.

beer and a detached radar unit in the car "exactly as I found it."

...The suspension order given Hawkins by Police Chief Warren Dodson...claims Hawkins violated Civil Service rules and regulations by acts of incompetency, neglect of duty, and conduct showing lack of good character, all stemming from an incident November 15.

...Officer H.D. Price said that when he came to work on the morning of Nov. 15, he found four cans of Schlitz beer in the back seat of the patrol car he normally drives. He also found part of the car's radar unit out of place on the front floorboard... Price notified his supervisor, Sgt. Jack Hurst, who called in a police photographer to record the conditions of the car as he found them.

Hurst testified that he checked the work sheet and found Hawkins was the officer who had driven the car last. He also said he found that Hawkins had arrested two men for public intoxication early that morning.

The charges against Hawkins stem from a letter he wrote shift commander Capt. E.L. O'Dell on Nov. 17 stating that he left the car exactly as he found it except for moving the beer from the front floorboard to the back seat.

According to Asst. Police Chief Dwain Pyburn, the two officers who used the car before Hawkins, Jimmy Seals and Larry Frymire, said they left the car relatively clean with the radar unit in place and with no beer inside it at the end of their shift on the night of Nov. 14...

In other testimony, Crispin Villarreal...said that an officer arrested him and his brother, Roberto, late Nov. 14 for public intoxication. He said they had four cans of beer in their car when stopped by the officer...after being arrested, someone put the beer in the back seat of the patrol car where he (Villarreal) was sitting, but he said he did not see who did it.

Pyburn...when he first heard about the matter, he thought it routine...But after conducting a personnel investigation, including discussion with the Villarreal brothers, Seals and Frymire, he concluded Hawkins was not telling the truth...he asked Capt. O'Dell what he would do if a man did not tell the truth in an official report. He said O'Dell replied, "I'd fire the bastard."

...Pyburn said he did not believe it significant enough to fire a man for having beer in a patrol car or a radar unit out of place.

He said the significant thing, to him, was submission of a false official report, apparently referring to Hawkins's Nov. 17 letter.

Exoneration

On Wednesday, January 5, 1977, Officer Bill Hawkins was exonerated of lying about the circumstances on November 15, 1976. The following information is from *The Abilene Reporter News,* Thursday Evening, Jan 6, 1977, page 3-A, entitled, *Officer to be given fresh start,* also by Ann Flores, Staff Writer:

> Commission chairman Charles Erwin said the commission found untrue accusations that Hawkins lied a about the circumstances of a Nov 15 incident in whih (sic) four cans of beer and a dismantled radar unit were found in the patrol car he had been driving...
>
> During the hearing, Dodson and Asst. Chief Dwain Pyburn testified that the presence of beer and a dismantled radar unit in the car were not the main reasons behind Hawkins' suspension. The bottom line, said Dodson, was that he had concluded that Hawkins was lying in official explanations he made Nov 17 and Nov 23. The suspension came two days after Hawkins failed to show up for the polygraph test ordered by Pyburn.
>
> Hawkins testified that he had been willing to take a polygraph test from an independent examiner, but did not want to take one administered by the Department of Public Safety as police proposed.
>
> After the suspension, Hawkins took two polygraph tests, both from independent examiners.
>
> Thad Johnson of Waco, who gave him a polygraph test Dec

7, testified that test results showed Hawkins was telling the truth when asked five questions about the incident previously posed by police.

Johnson, who was hired by Cockerell to administer the test, said Hawkins was very cooperative, which he called a big part of the test.

The following day, Hawkins took another polygraph test set up by the police department and administered by Glynn Gibson of Odessa. According to a deposition from Gibson, the results of that test were inconclusive.

Hawkins testified that he was nervous during the second test because he had seen Pyburn talking to Gibson beforehand and could hear Pyburn's voice during the test. Hawkins said he felt the case against him was built up by Pyburn because of ill will the assistant chief bore him for not buying a mobile home from Pyburn several years ago.

Charges Found to be True

However, other accusations against Bill were found to be true. From this same article on page 3-A in the Thursday Evening, Jan 6, 1977, issue of *The Abilene Reporter News,* this reads:

> After a full day of testimony Wednesday, the commission found Hawkins guilty of four charges made by Dodson alleging that he willfully disobeyed an order and neglected his duty...
>
> The commission found true Dodson's charge that Hawkins willfully disobeyed an order from Asst. Chief Dwain Pyburn to take a polygraph (lie detector) test in the case Nov 26. Pyburn said Hawkins failed to show up at the assigned time.
>
> Also found true by the commission were charges that Hawkins neglected his duty by failing to "book" the beer in as evidence, by failing to place the radar unit in its proper place and by failing to notify his superiors that the radar was out of place.
>
> After hearing Hawkins' appeal Wednesday, the Civil Service Commission ordered a 30-day suspension retroactively effective

Nov 28. That period would have elapsed Dec 28, meaning Hawkins can return to work immediately...

Police Chief Warren Dodson said today he has reassigned Officer Bill Hawkins...to a different patrol company to "give him a fresh start..."

Dodson, who had sought to have his indefinite suspension of Hawkins continued, said he would not appeal the commission decision.

He said he reassigned Hawkins this morning to Company A under Capt. George McGee's command and ordered to report for work to his new captain today. Hawkins previously served in Company B under Capt. E.L. O'Dell.

Hawkins could not be reached after his talk with Dodson to say when he would return, although earlier this morning he said he would prefer to return to work Sunday. Hawkins' attorney, Ed Cockerell, said today he does not know whether his client will appeal although he said both he and Hawkins are unhappy with the commission's decision.

Cockerell said Hawkins' case would be almost laughable if it were not tragic. "There's more than one way to skin a cat." He remarked, saying it appears police officials made a "mountain out of a molehill."

Other Officers Implicated

In the Thursday Morning, January 6, 1977, issue of *The Abilene Reporter News,* Page 6-C, written by Ann Flores, Staff Writer, it was revealed that the two officers who had driven the patrol car before Bill had been temporarily suspended for five days for the same incident. This was the first time this had been revealed. The news media did not even find out about this until this hearing. These men and their families had been spared the pain and humiliation that I had endured.

In the article entitled, *Suspension of Two Officers Revealed,* this information is given:

Two other Abilene police officers were temporarily suspended in connection with an incident for which patrolman Bill Hawkins was indefinitely suspended Nov 28, it was revealed Wednesday. Officers Jimmy Seals and Larry Frymire were suspended for five days each and allowed to work it off without pay for taking four cans of beer which were found Nov 15 inside the patrol car they drove the day before. Hawkins used the same car during the shift immediately following theirs in the early morning hours of Nov 15. Both Seals and Frymire told the Civil Service Commission Wednesday the beer was not in the car when they left it the night of Nov 14. They said they first noticed the beer in the sergeant's office at the police station before going on duty the next day. The beer had been taken out of the patrol car that day by Sgt. Jack Hurst after Officer H.D. Price reported finding it in the car when he went to get in it.

Seals and Frymire said that several fellow officers, knowing that the pair had driven the car the day before, began kidding them about the beer when they arrived for work Nov 15. They said no one had claimed the beer and it was not marked for evidence, so they took it and hid it in the snow outside the police station.

Frymire said that when they got off duty that night Seals asked him if he wanted to take the beer home. He said he replied no, whereupon Seals took the beer home with him. They said they later confessed separately to their superiors and were given the temporary suspensions.

Reinstatement

Bill returned to work that night. *The Abilene Reporter News* ran the article entitled, *Officer feels good on return to work,* in the Friday Evening edition of the newspaper dated Jan 7, 1977, page 5-A, by Ann Flores:

Police Officer Bill Hawkins returned to work on the midnight shift Thursday, saying he felt "really good" about resuming his duties as a patrolman.

Letter of Resignation

One week later a news conference was convened, at which time Bill publicly resigned from the Abilene Police Department and submitted his Letter of Resignation. Excerpts from the Front Page article entitled, *Reinstated policeman Hawkins resigns,* in the Wednesday Evening, January 12, 1977, edition of *The Abilene Reporter News,* no byline, state:

> Police Officer Bill Hawkins...reinstated by the Civil Service Commission just last week, resigned today because of what he called "time consuming personal business interests."
>
> The nine-year officer said he had planned to resign several months ago but postponed his plans when he was indefinitely suspended Nov 28 by Police Chief Warren Dodson...
>
> He said he knew after being suspended "that I must delay my resignation and fight to preserve my integrity." Hawkins said in his resignation letter given to Dodson this morning.
>
> "Now that the Civil Service Commission has found that the charges that I lied are untrue, I can submit my resignation with dignity," he said...
>
> Hawkins said he plans to devote full time now to his business interests...(which)...include AAA Mobile Home Park...about 50 rent houses...and a new mobile home park he plans to develop soon at T&P Lane and Midway.

Bill and I had repeatedly talked about him resigning from the police department, but it did not occur. After Bill was suspended, I knew that Bill must fight this in order to preserve his name and honor. If Buffalo Bill Hawkins had not been exonerated of the charges leveled against him, Bill's future would have taken an entirely different course. There are events which have changed the course of history. This event changed the course of our lives. At the time I did not realize that as a policeman Bill had opportunities to be constantly excited and stimulated. I did not understand that once Bill left this environment, that he would seek other means to indulge his senses.

After the trial and Bill's resignation, our lives started to get back to normal. Bill requested and received his accumulated deposits into the Texas Municipal Retirement System and paid his legal fees. We rented out our house in Abilene, and focused on growing our rent business and our farming interests. We attended weekly Sabbaths, the Feast of Passover and Unleavened Bread and Pentecost with The Worldwide Church of God, while continuing our visits with Jacob and his family in Odessa, Texas.

The Worldwide Church of God, Abilene, by this time was led by Elder Harold Smith, a very dedicated, conscientious, young pastor and educator. I was blessed that he was the leader of the congregation. There were bible studies every Wednesday night during which I was taught wonderful things about the Law, Prophets, and Writings. I understood everything that was being taught. I felt that I had received my "high school education" in the study of The Holy Scriptures. This was a very fulfilling spiritual year.

However, this was the year that we experienced our first business failure. One of the first things we built on our farm in 1977 was a large chicken house which would hold two hundred birds. We ordered two hundred baby chicks in the spring and brooded them. When the pullets got about six weeks old, we put them in our new chicken house and trained them to get on the roost at night. The only problem was there was not a pen built to contain the birds outside during the day, so they went everywhere.

I asked Bill to construct a pen, but he said that he liked to see the pullets walking around. This was fine until the chickens began laying eggs early that summer and, since they were not penned, they also laid them wherever they wanted. I knew by experience that this was not the way to raise chickens, but Bill would not listen to me.

Our first egg market was to a local fast food restaurant. They were not satisfied because the eggs were too small. Bill sold our next egg market to the Clyde Elementary school, and then he immediately made plans to take our annual vacation on Padre Island at the end of July.

I told Bill we couldn't go since we had this business to take care of. Bill told me not to worry about it because he had already made arrangements with our park manager, Mrs. Oakley, and her daughter to take care of the chickens while we were gone. To make a long story short, this daughter and her children discovered some of the eggs that were rotten and put them with the fresh eggs that were sent to the school. They had never been around chickens and they didn't know the difference. Needless to say, our egg business was ruined.

We then had a huge sale to get rid of the young hens. We would continue to raise a few chickens, but never again on a commercial level. This was also the first time I saw Bill start something and then begin to neglect it when the excitement wore off and the day to day maintenance became boring. This would not be the last time this cycle would continue.

Marriage

On August 1, 1977, Bill and I finally got married. We were again vacationing on Padre Island in South Texas and attending services with The Worldwide Church of God in Corpus Christi. Bill did not want to get married by any preacher, especially one from The Worldwide Church of God. He also wanted to be married in the "Name of Yahweh."

The Justice of the Peace of Refugio County agreed to preside. It is significant that during our marriage ceremony, and by his own free will, Bill "vowed" to me, by affirming in the "Name of Yahweh" to "forsake all others and keep himself only unto me." These words are from the Texas Official Handbook for Justices of the Peace, which were the words read to us during our ceremony. A man is only as good as his word, and at the time I believed that Bill would honor his "vow."

As soon as we returned from our vacation, we began to build our new house at Eula. This project was started in August, 1977, and occupied our time until it was completed.

CHAPTER FIVE

1978
Sorrow upon Sorrow upon Sorrow

The year 1978 began with warm weather at the beginning of January, but I will remember this year as one of sorrow and distress, personally and spiritually. Our new home was completed and furnished by the end of January, 1978, and our House Warming was scheduled February 5th. The whole Abilene congregation of The Worldwide Church came, as did Mother and Daddy. Bill's brother and wife from Graham, Texas, also attended. We had a wonderful celebration.

Afterward, Bill seemed lost. He wanted to do nothing but go to our mobile home park. There was plowing and all other kinds of work that could have been done, but he personally lost interest in keeping up the farm. Bill tried to get Dennis to drive the tractor to do the plowing, but I absolutely refused to allow this. Dennis was around eleven-years-old and this type of work was too dangerous. So, Bill delegated specific farm chores to our children, milking cows and raising chickens.

The fields were not plowed, so the few cows we had grazed on what grew voluntarily. The hay field grew up into a mesquite tree pasture, and the cultivated fields grew up into sunflowers. The farm equipment was idle. I made butter and cheese, raised a garden and canned the produce. I also cooked three meals a day and did the bookkeeping for our business, AAA Mobile Home Park.

Bill then became filled with rage and hatred against everyone that I seemed to have any respect for. He became the most negative person

I had ever known. He criticized everyone and everything. He was paranoid and thought everyone was out to get him.

Until this time I would not have believed that such an inferiority complex could have existed. I would later learn that it was not only an inferiority complex that haunted him, it was a much more complex mental condition.

Bill was a successful businessman and had so much to be thankful for. In order to help Bill overcome these self-defeating traits and come to an understanding that people are just people regardless of their status, I suggested and urged Bill to enroll in a popular speech class. This began on February 20, 1978, and ended on May 22. Bill attended class every week and regularly came home with trophies and personal acknowledgements.

I thought Bill was heading in the right direction. His mood lightened up. He began to be aware how "power" clothing "made the man," and purchased a light gray three-piece-suit to reflect his new self-image. He met other business men and women and seemed to be overcoming much of his negativity and paranoia.

It was on Mother's Day in the spring of 1978 that Mother announced that she was scheduled for surgery. The next week, the surgeon told Daddy, me, my sisters and my brother that Mother had level-4 adeno-carcinoma of the colon, that it had already metastasized, and that she had about two years to live. Mother was fifty-eight-years old. I had turned thirty. All of us were crushed at the news. "What about chemotherapy or radiation?" we asked the surgeon. "No, the colon was very resistant to this type of treatment." No hope was given to us.

As Mother was rousing from anesthesia, each of us went in to speak to her. "Yes, Mother, you have a colostomy, but you can live with that." No one told Mother her grim prognosis.

From that time forward my thoughts were with my mother and with trying to find a way to help her recover. I remember the round of working on my farm during the week, going to Saturday services at The Worldwide Church of God, then driving to Royston every Sunday to see Mother. She slowly began to get her strength back and become more like her old self. Of course, none of us had told our mother that her days were numbered. None of us had wanted to believe it either.

About the same time that I learned my mother was dying of colon cancer was about the same time that I found out that Bill was keeping regular company with a woman who had also enrolled in same speaking class that he did. The first time I met her was when the whole group came for a hot dog party at our new house to celebrate the class graduation, and she was just "one of the hostesses."

She was a recent divorcee with children. Bill suddenly became involved with the work that she did and, of course, was only promoting charity and good works. To me, this was a really hollow, flimsy excuse. Bill did not have a charitable bone in his body until then, so this behavior was completely out of character. He had to be with her for board meetings and press releases; so innocent yet so time-consuming. Bill was away from the house for long periods of time.

Bill also told me that I was the one who wanted him to go to speech class in the first place, so now it was my fault that he had met her.

My thoughts were on Mother and how I could help her. My thoughts were not on Buffalo Bill Hawkins and what he might be doing behind my back. During our marriage ceremony, remember, Bill had "vowed" to me in the "Name of Yahweh" to forsake all others and keep himself only unto me? I would only learn later what a liar, a manipulator, and a con-artist this man really is—and that his "word" means nothing.

It was on Sabbath, June 24, 1978, that Herbert W. Armstrong declared a day of fasting and prayer for The Worldwide Church of God. According to John Tuit, author of *The Truth Shall Make You Free,*

> "…The calling of a fast by Herbert Armstrong was always an effective way to cause the Church membership to feel as though they were responsible for the problems in the Church. Armstrong, of course, never did anything wrong. The reasons for the problems were always, according to him, a result of God withdrawing His blessings from the Church due to the spiritual laxity on the part of the membership…this entire matter of a fast was part of a conditioning process to prepare the membership for the next event…an announcement…would be made to the membership the following Sabbath…"[8]

---

8   *The Truth Will Make You Free,* Copyright© 1981 by John Tuit, The Truth Foundation, 11 Laurel Court, Freehold Township, New Jersey 07758, page 93.

Garner Ted Armstrong, Herbert W. Armstrong's only surviving son, was marked before the church and disfellowshipped![9]

I thought to myself, "How could a father do that to his own son?" Herbert W. Armstrong became fully committed to keeping his death grip on power and control. This marked the point that began an unending barrage of worship for Herbert W. Armstrong over the pulpit. I can still hear it in my mind:

> Herbert W was putting the church back on track as the ONLY TRUE CHURCH, and he, as God's ONLY APOSTLE, was being used to do it.[10]

The Heavenly Father and His Only Begotten Son were forgotten so praise could be heaped upon Herbert W. Armstrong. He would sacrifice anybody and anything. His only surviving son was only one of the casualties.

Buffalo Bill Hawkins studied Armstrong's tactics carefully.

Another casualty of the power struggle taking place at that time was Elder Harold Smith. He was replaced suddenly, without notice. The distinguished Elder Gerald Waterhouse of Pasadena, California, had been banished to West Texas, and the Abilene and San Angelo congregations were the benefactors. I actually heard these long winded sermons about fleeing to Petra as the Place of Safety.[11]

Gerald Waterhouse had it all worked out; people would sell their homes and contribute the money to the "Petra fund." Gerald spoke of Stanley Rader, Armstrong's attorney, purchasing DC-10 planes with 10-inch cracks that God would cover with 11-inch angels. Church members from all over the world would be transported to Jerusalem,

---

9   *The Truth Will Make You Free*, Tuit, page 95.

10   *The Truth Will Make Your Free*, Tuit, Page 118. Thanks to *Restitution of All Things* website, www.keithhunt.com, for making Mr.Tuit's book available for reading on-line.

11   *Herbert Armstrong's Tangled Web*, Copyright© 1980 by David Robinson, John Hadden Publishers, P.O. Box 35982, Tulsa, Oklahoma 74135, page 238. Thanks to Exit & Support Network, refuge@frii.com, for being able to quote excerpts, page numbers, etc. from the books I have. Thanks also to Des Griffin of *Emissary Publications*, 9205 SE Clackamas Rd, #1776, Clackamas, OR 97015, (503) 824-2050, who also gave permission to print excerpts of *The Truth Shall Make You Free* and *Herbert Armstrong's Tangled Webb*.

then to Tekoa, a Jerusalem suburb. The Worldwide Church members would build a highway to Petra, in Jordan. According to Gerald, the European countries would think that Herbert W. Armstrong had come down with an army to take over the Middle Eastern oil fields and would send down armies to capture them. God would destroy the European armies. The earth would swallow them up and the church would march triumphantly down to Petra, while Herbert W. drove back and forth from Jerusalem in his Rolls Royce attending to the business of being one of "Two Witnesses."[12] Christ's return would not be far off.

We were hearing the same sermon of "fables" from Gerald Waterhouse every Sabbath day. Gerald didn't have any other sermon that he was able to preach. At the beginning of every sermon Gerald would announce the greatness of Herbert W. Armstrong, that we had—

"... been called to Christ, to His Work, to His headquarters, to His Apostle..."[13]

"...Mr. Armstrong could be 95% wrong, and...Ted could be 95% right and it is still a matter of government. God still backs up Mr. Armstrong. I don't care if he's 99% wrong on a point."[14]

The Petra Sermon immediately followed the praise of Herbert W. Armstrong. Gerald preached in the mornings at the San Angelo branch of the congregation, where four hour sermons were common. At least, when he got to Abilene he was almost winded; his sermons here only lasted about two hours.

Crude rumors were also beginning to fly out of Pasadena about Herbert W. Armstrong and Stanley Rader.[15] Letters also flew to the members of The Worldwide Church of God in which Herbert W. would close with the fact that our increased financial support was urgent. The following quotations from John Tuit's book clearly state the situation going on at the time,

"We are moving with THE WORK swiftly! I need your

---

12 *Herbert Armstrong's Tangled Web,* Robinson, page 239-240.

13 *Herbert Armstrong's Tangled Web,* Robinson, page 228.

14 *Herbert Armstrong's Tangled Web,* Robinson, page 229.

15 *The Truth Shall Make You Free,* by John Tuit, pages 253-260, Chapter 19 entitled "Blackmail?"

earnest prevailing, believing PRAYERS. We need INCREASED FINANCIAL SUPPORT! IT IS URGENT. THANK YOU IN JESUS' NAME…This type of communication from Herbert W. Armstrong is typical of the continuing propaganda efforts to which we were subjected…It was to be some time before I would come to realize that Paula and I had become part of a church that was in the final states of being perverted into one of the most diabolically controlled organizations in existence."[16]

That is, until The House of Yahweh, Abilene, as it is today. This went on for months. I was tired of the monotony of propaganda. I was afraid for my mother. I was being deceived by my husband who was being "only friends" with another woman. I felt hopeless.

The Feast of Tabernacles was again kept by us at Big Sandy, Texas, from October 16-23, 1978. This was the first time that I had personally seen Stanley Rader. He had accompanied Herbert W. to one of the morning services, during which he gave a very boring speech. I remember there was increased security during this short interval. My impression of Stanley was that he did not have the ability to inspire or to lead. They both left early that afternoon. At least during this feast I did not have to compete with Bill's "friend." She was not a member of the church.

On November 18, 1978, the Jonestown Massacre took place in Guyana, South America. There were over 900 victims; men, women, and children who drank the grape flavored drink laced with cyanide. I remember that a sermonette was brought the following Sabbath about this incident—that this would reflect negatively on the image of The Worldwide Church of God.

A short time after the Jonestown Suicide, Gerald Waterhouse was called back from exile in West Texas. He was needed by headquarters to proclaim "total loyalty" to Herbert W. Armstrong in another state.

In Gerald Waterhouse's place, headquarters sent another minister to Abilene; a young, single man by the name of Elder Mark Robinson.

It was about this same time, early winter of 1978, that Bill's "friend" and her children began sitting with us during weekly Sabbath services of The Worldwide Church of God. It would have been acceptable if she had sat by herself with her children, but that was not the case. Mrs. Oakley and her daughter sat behind us during these services and I did

16 *The Truth Shall Make You Free*, Tuit, Page 28.

not feel threatened. I thought, "How could my husband do this to me?" When I confronted Bill about this, he said, "No, she is being called by God, so how could this be wrong? Do you want her to lose her eternal life because of you? She's only sitting with us."

Bill might have thought that this was just fine, but this was not just fine with me. Everyone else in the congregation also took note. About this same time Bill convinced the young Elder Robinson that it would be a great idea to start a Spokesmen Club. This would sharpen the speaking skills of the men who might be interested in that sort of thing.

Coincidentally, at around the same time-frame, Bill decided that he needed an office at our mobile home park, so he purchased a portable building and converted it into his private office. This was so much more convenient for him to watch over our business and for studying his speech assignments, or so he said.

Now it was December and Christmas was around the corner and this poor woman and her children would be missing Christmas for the first time. Bill said that they really needed spiritual support to get through this. I thought to myself, "What spiritual support did you give me the first time I did not keep Christmas? Oh, I remember, you stated that we were not going to keep Christmas, we were not going to buy any toys for the children, and we could not even go visit my family."

Bill invited them, and they came to my house where we did not keep Christmas. I didn't like this at all, and I told Bill about it. "This doesn't look right. This woman needs to seek the company of a single man if that is what she wants, and Bill, you are not a single man." "No, no, no, it's not like that. She's my sister in the faith and we need to help her as much as we can."

I don't know if you have ever been in a circumstance like this, but it is frustratingly impossible to reason with someone who does not have the mental capacity to even understand the consequences of his actions.[17] This is what I had to deal with. I was thirty-years-old and felt powerless. Bill was determined that he was "doing nothing wrong,"[18] so he continued to do it regardless of how I felt about it.

---

17 *Take Back Your Life, Recovering from Cults and Abusive Relationships,* by Janja Lalich and Madeleine Tobias (Bay Tree Publishing LLC, Pt. Richmond, CA. www.baytreepublishing.com) pages 65-66 under "Irresponsibility and Unreliability." Used with permission.

18 *Take Back Your Life,* page 63 under "Lack of Remorse, Shame, and Guilt"

I thought about not writing about this time in my life and spare the feelings of the innocent who will probably be reading this one day, but this episode must be written in order to reveal Bill's twisted mentality; a perverted mindset that will not allow him to change his ways, will not allow him to learn from his mistakes, and refuses to believe that he has committed any sin or wrong-doing by his actions. [19] My mistake was that of not understanding this fact at the time. I would not repeat this same error in judgment again.

---

19   *Take Back Your Life,* page 63 under "Lack of Remorse, Shame, and Guilt"

Chapter Six

1979
The End of The Worldwide Church of God

On January 3, 1979, the Attorney General seized control of The Worldwide Church of God Headquarters in Pasadena, California. A class-action lawsuit was filed against the leadership of The Worldwide Church of God to force them to give account for how the *millions of dollars of tithes* were being spent. The first press release from Herbert W. Armstrong, dated January 3, 1979, seemed to indicate that he was going to do the right thing. This Press Release stated:

> I have been shocked beyond measure to learn of the raid on our executive offices in Pasadena this morning, initiated from the State of California Attorney General's office. I know little of the facts as yet. The Worldwide Church of God and Ambassador College are both upstanding institutions and we are people of integrity.
>
> If any improprieties have existed in either institution, I want them to be known, and I shall take every effort to cooperate with the Attorney General's office. We are an institution of 46 years' standing. We have many departments and branch offices around the world. We employ many hundreds. I have of necessity had to entrust responsibilities to various officers under me. I am appointing Mr. C. Wayne Cole as Acting Chief Executive Officer under me till this crisis has passed. Mr.

Cole is Director of Pastoral Administration over our ministry worldwide. Signed, Herbert W. Armstrong[20]

The Right Thing—which was actually a move to try to save The Worldwide Church of God from total destruction through corruption and self-dealing—did not prevail.[21]

C. Wayne Cole and others appointed by Herbert W. Armstrong, who could have resolved this sordid mess in Pasadena, California, and who could have saved The Worldwide Church of God—were marked and disfellowshipped![22]

The men who insinuated themselves to DESTROY the church gained complete control.[23]

Every righteous thing that The Worldwide Church of God previously stood for was now in question. The backwater of Abilene, Texas, would not be free of this contamination. If only the weekly Sabbath sermons thereafter were filled with the praise of the Heavenly Father instead of Herbert W. Armstrong, there might have been hope.

Instead, propaganda was spewed to the congregations in the form of taped sermons, relentless in denigrating the church takeover, and boundless in propagating loyalty and obedience to one selfish, greedy, power-hungry, old man.

My birthday was coming up at the end of January. Bill told me that he would like to take me out to Buffalo Gap Steakhouse for dinner, but since January 28, 1979, fell on a Saturday this year it would be better to go out on Friday night, January 27. When we arrived we were led to a table that held two huge bouquets of red roses, with Bill's "friend" already seated there. Bill had a huge grin on his face. I could not believe what I was seeing. Bill had not said one word to me about "her" being there. Of course, if he had I would not have gone out with him.

On reflection, I should have picked up one of the vases holding a bouquet of red roses, and poured it over Bill's head as I walked out the door. I would have left both of them to each other. But I didn't. I was

---

20 *The Truth Shall Make You Free*, John Tuit, page 199. A facsimile copy of this Press Release is also found in *Herbert Armstrong's Tangled Web*, David Robinson, Appendix iv.

21 *Herbert Armstrong's Tangled Web*, Robinson, page 180.

22 *Herbert Armstrong's Tangled Web*, Robinson, page 181.

23 *Herbert Armstrong's Tangled Web*, Robinson, page 186.

thirty-one-years old and felt betrayed, miserable, helpless, angry, and alone. Bill refused to accept the fact that his girlfriend was a problem and a deep pain to me. According to him, I was the one who had the problem.

This was just one more way that Buffalo Bill Hawkins got away with manipulation, lying, and deceit. A tiger cannot change his stripes, and when he tried this same tactic on me again, many years later, I did not behave as compliantly.

I was unable to take this problem with Bill to the Elders of The Worldwide Church; I was manipulated into believing that it would be shameful to talk about my husband to other men, so I felt guilty for even considering it. I couldn't take this problem to my parents, since my mother was fighting cancer and I wouldn't burden her. I took my problem to Isabel Hawkins via telephone. Isabel was sympathetic but not any real help. It was only much later that she confessed about her own ordeals with Jacob playing around, committing fornication and adultery with other women all the time they were married.

Bill convinced himself that he was becoming a very powerful man in The Worldwide Church of God, Abilene, when young, single Mark Robinson became the pastor. In the spring of 1979, Bill convinced Mark that it would be better to cater the dinner on the Night to be Much Observed, rather than everyone going to a public restaurant meeting room.

When the time came, the regular meeting hall for Sabbath services was set up with tables and chairs, and the front tables were ready for the food to be delivered. The caterers were cafeteria workers from another church. I looked with amazement as they brought in their cooking pots filled with food, set them on the serving tables, then left. It might have been nicer if their cooking pots and utensils were made of stainless steel, but they weren't. What a disaster.

Everyone was dressed in their nicest clothing at a religious function, and we were fishing green beans from a four-gallon graniteware pot using a wood handled, slotted spoon with chipped paint.

Bill did not ask for my suggestions when arranging this event, but here I was, standing by this man whom I felt had just made a fool out of himself as a credible, responsible leader. This would not be the end of Bill's grasp for power under the leadership of young Elder Mark Robinson.

The Spokesmen's Club continued to meet on a weekly basis, and Bill Hawkins was one of its most promising students. It was decided that there would be a class graduation to celebrate their completion and to display their speaking skills to their family members. It was decided by the class that Bill Hawkins make the arrangements to secure a meeting room and arrange for the food service, which, I learned later, was to be according to individual choices from the menu.

As usual, Bill procrastinated. At the last minute he realized that the Spokesmen's graduation was scheduled during the same time that the Abilene Independent School District had their graduations, and almost every meeting room in Abilene was already reserved. The only room available was at the Royale Inn, and the only food service was a group menu, not individual choices. Bill could have met with the class the next Sabbath and could have arranged to postpone the graduation for the next week, but Bill did not want to apologize.

Instead, he took it upon himself to reserve the only meeting room remaining in Abilene that weekend and to order KC steaks for everyone. Bill and I arrived early, and Bill's "friend" was waiting for us in the room, smiling. I felt like I had been punched in the stomach. He did not tell me that "she" would be here.

As couples began to arrive, I heard some pointed discussions about the food arrangement. Bill had a glazed stare on his face and acted like everything was just fine. I quickly realized Bill's manipulation of the situation and felt angry, ashamed, and embarrassed.

The tables were already set up for the food service and the steaks were coming in. It was a good thing that ordering a beer with dinner was accepted in The Worldwide Church of God. I ordered one and I quickly ordered another. After this ordeal was over, Bill was stuck with a food charge of over $200.00. There was a stack of steaks on a platter at the head table. I don't know who got them. I couldn't wait to get out of there.

Now that Bill was a graduate of the Spokesmen's Club, his Song Leading responsibility under Mark Robinson grew into that of preaching a mini-sermonette every Sabbath morning. Bill received Elder Mark Robinson's approval, or this would not have been allowed.

I remember the first time I heard Bill's mini-sermonette. He talked about Psalm 19 and it having three parts, and the first was God's revelation of Himself in His material works and the meaning was outer space and the world globe. While he was speaking, I was dying of embarrassment as I sat at the piano, praying for him to shut up. He didn't warn me in advance that he was going to do this, and he sounded pompous and arrogant.

During the week Bill had plenty of free time on his hands to study Jacob's literature. We both studied and agreed upon the correct way to count Pentecost: the Jews kept Pentecost-Shavout on any day of the week upon which it fell, not "always on Sunday." Bill and I had already studied the Name of Yahweh in Jacob's literature. I agreed that Yahweh did have a Name, and that it was honorable to use.

There were things that we did not accept as we studied with Jacob: The concept of a completely kosher kitchen with the separation of meat and milk was not proven from the scripture to be a law of Yahweh; it was a tradition accepted by the Jews. Men were required to grow a beard. Men were required to wear a kippah and women were required to wear a head-covering, at all times.

During the week Bill also had all the time he needed to pursue his own entertainment. In the summer of 1979, Bill took several fishing trips with our children to Lake Comanche and to Lake O.H. Ivie. My son, years later, informed me that Bill would purchase large amounts of food and soft-drinks, leave the children under the care of his right hand man, and then completely vanish for several days.

Afterward, Bill would arrive to get everyone and take them back to Abilene. Bill made frequent trips like this all during the time he had "her" as a "friend."

Bill's good works continued. This time he became a publicity director and promoted contests which were published in the media. At another time a small pig had been donated; Bill reported that the pig had been stolen and signed an affidavit to its loss with the police department. He then notified the local news and radio stations. Bill wanted this information broadcast far and wide. I could not believe what I was hearing.

The members of The Worldwide Church of God did not eat pork, and here was Bill Hawkins, the Song Leader of the congregation, openly playing around with a pig.

Bill did not understand the implications of this image. When I tried to explain to him how this looked, he glibly dismissed my concern. "This is not something that a responsible leader of The Worldwide Church of God would be doing," I explained. He did not seem to care what they thought. This was not the last time that Bill would have complete disregard for the negative image that he was portraying.

The Feast of Tabernacles, 1979, would not be held at Big Sandy, Texas, this year. Herbert W. Armstrong had set out to liquidate the printing assets in Pasadena, California, as well as the church's land holdings. Big Sandy, Texas, was on the auction block.[24] Herbert W. Armstrong and Stanley Rader had set out to gut the financial foundation of The Worldwide Church of God, and it was being accomplished in a systematic manner.

It was announced to the local congregation that there were different feast sites available, and one of them was in Tucson, Arizona, set for October 6 through 13, 1979.

Bill and I were becoming more and more affiliated with Jacob Hawkins and The House of Yahweh, Odessa, and less concerned with The Worldwide Church of God, which was a dying religious institution. We decided to keep the Feast of Tabernacles with The House of Yahweh in Odessa, Texas, and also with The Worldwide Church of God in Tucson, Arizona.

Bill and I reserved rooms in The House of Yahweh Building for us and our children, and also for his "friend" and her children. I fully expected to hear from Jacob Hawkins that bringing a single woman with Bill would not be the proper thing to do, but I heard no such thing.

Bill and I also reserved a roundtrip flight to Tucson, Arizona, and a motel room for three nights. We drove to Odessa and set up our rooms, keeping the first part of the Feast of Tabernacles with The House of Yahweh in Odessa. In the middle of the week we left The House of Yahweh, with our children under the "friend's" care, and caught our flight to Arizona from the Midland International Airport.

Bill and I showed our faces just two times to the Abilene congregation

---

24 *The Truth Shall Make You Free,* John Tuit, page 186.

in that huge auditorium, but we did not remain for any sermon. It was going to be "Praise Herbert W. Armstrong," and we had already heard enough of that. Bill and I rented a car and drove around Arizona, visiting Kitt Peak National Observatory, a saguaro cactus grove, Old Tucson which was a movie set, and several other places.

We then flew back to Odessa, where we celebrated the remainder of the feast days and our oldest son's Bar Mitzvah, since Dennis was now thirteen-years-old.

After our return to Abilene, Bill's prestige slowly began to decline. There are scriptures in the bible that speak of taking your place in the back of the room, and when you are asked to come to the front there will be honor. Bill took his place in the front seat for a little while. It was a sad and disappointing day when he was told to go and sit down at the back of the room.

David Robinson, Elder Mark Robinson's father, was a long-time member and Elder of The Worldwide Church of God. He was forced out, expelled by Herbert W. Armstrong in 1979. Since that time Mark had been under suspicion, and it was only a matter of time before he would also have to go. Bill was on the wrong side of the power struggle.

It would have been about November of 1979, that Lyle Greaves assumed Mark's position as Elder of The Worldwide Church of God, Abilene. At the same time, Bill's power eroded. No longer was there a mini-sermonette before each Sabbath song service. All the material that was brought to the congregation had to be reviewed for official church doctrine. Lyle was not as personable as Mark, and not easily flattered.

Bill would still get dressed and drive to his office in Abilene. He was still involved with "her" at the time, but Bill had lost his game with Lyle. He was unable to charm and influence him. Bill became more agitated and angry, and turned more and more to Jacob for approval.

It was at this point that Bill began in earnest to study Jacob's literature, and absorb the portions that suited him as his own.

Chapter Seven

1980
Dedication of the Mobile Sanctuary

M y mother's health began to rapidly fail at the beginning of 1980. She continued to lose weight each weekend that we saw her. There came a time in late March, 1980, that she was unable to eat anything. This is when she asked to go to the hospital in Rotan, Texas. My sisters and I took turns staying with Mother in the hospital. Bill had bought a Coachman travel trailer, and he stayed in it on the hospital grounds when it was my turn.

The Feast of Unleavened Bread was scheduled from April 1 through April 7, 1980, so I also focused on buying clothes and preparing for this. Mother's sixtieth birthday was on April 28, 1980. She remained hospitalized, sedated from excruciating pain, until her death on the morning of May 20, 1980. That same day, Dad, my three sisters, my brother, and I arranged for her funeral the next day, May 21, 1980. When I left Mother's graveside on that day, I was thirty-two-years old. It would be fifteen years later before I was mentally able to return.

In order to block the pain of Mother's death, I focused my energy and attention on my children, my religion, and my businesses.

Bill studied the subject of "Pentecost," which he received from Jacob. We had come to the conclusion that the Jews were keeping this feast correctly, and that Herbert Armstrong and The Worldwide Church of God was not. However, this difference in belief did not prevent us from showing up at Armstrong's Pentecost on Sunday, May 18. Bill still wanted to speak in Armstrong's organization. He was also still the song leader at the time. We did not attend the Feast of Pentecost at The House of Yahweh in Odessa in 1980—Mother's death and funeral occurred during the time this took place.

During the summer Bill took me on a road trip out west, while our children stayed with "her."

Then suddenly, Bill just stopped going to church. I asked him why. He told me that he was not allowed to preach about the "Name of Yahweh." This is what Bill told me. I have always had questions about this explanation. Armstrong never allowed the "Name of Yahweh" to be preached in his congregations, and Bill knew it. The only thing that changed was the fact that Bill was not attending church any longer, and I was no longer playing the piano during the song service.

I continued to go to services at The Worldwide Church of God for about two more Sabbaths, but realized that I was fed up with the praise of Armstrong. In 1980, David Robinson, Mark Robinson's father, published an expose entitled, *Herbert Armstrong's Tangled Web, An Insider's View of the Worldwide Church of God.*

When I read this book, I learned "why" Herbert W. Armstrong had marked and disfellowshipped his only surviving son. Quotes from this book follow,

Incest is a terrible and unnatural crime, an extreme perversity…Herbert Armstrong was, himself, guilty of this vile sin. I learned of this in the summer of 1979 from members of his own family…told in awful detail. One family source was Garner Ted Armstrong…in the spring of 1978 while in his father's house for the last time his father had threatened to "destroy him." Ted, in response, replied, "Dad, I will destroy you. I know about you and (…the younger of his two sisters.)" …Ted has told many people that there was a look in his father's eyes he had never seen before. Ted knew his father was now determined to totally destroy any credibility he might have. It was either him or his son…Such matters should not normally be mentioned but…The welfare of thousands is at stake, and thousands…look to HWA, idolizing him as if he were God… Now people must be given enough information to make an intelligent decision on whether this is the man who is going to lead them to safety during the "crisis at the close," or whether he is just going to continue taking their money and calling them "dumb sheep." [25]

After reading this book, I realized that The Worldwide Church of God under Herbert W. Armstrong was spiritually dead as a religious organization; but I loved the members of the church. They were my second family. My children played with their children. I was mentally torn.

Bill and I were studying about the "casting of lots" for making a decision, and contacted Jacob before proceeding. Bill then cast the lots. One was labeled "Worldwide Church," and the other was labeled "House of Yahweh." The lot chosen was "House of Yahweh." Sadly, we completely cut the cord to The Worldwide Church of God.

Bill, also suddenly, stopped seeing the "other woman" about this same time. I asked him what happened, but he said nothing. I remember him walking to the patio door and looking out with a long blank stare on his face. I still don't know what happened and have no reason to try to find out. Remarkably, this breakup didn't seem to affect Bill for very long. In a couple of days it was as though she had never existed to him. To me, it felt as though a heavy burden had been lifted.

We attended the Feast of Tabernacles at The House of Yahweh, Odessa. This would have been September 25 through October 2, 1980.

I was baptized during this feast by Jacob. Bill was ordained as an Elder in The House of Yahweh, Odessa, Texas.

Since Bill had broken off his relationship with "her" just before this feast, I justified Bill's election as an "Elder" in my mind. I convinced myself that if the Apostle Paul, who was once a murderer, could change, then Buffalo Bill Hawkins could also become a different man.

When Bill and I returned to Abilene we held the very first service of The House of Yahweh in my living room, October 9, 1980, attended by seven people—Bill, me, and our five children. We immediately bought an old mobile home set it up on our property facing Eula Highway 603 and refurbished it. Bill and I built the podium, bought new chairs,

---

25 *Herbert Armstrong's Tangled Web*, David Robinson, page 266.

and moved my childhood piano from my dad's house to the "mobile sanctuary."

The very first service in this place was the Feast of Dedication, December 2, 1980, at which time Jacob and Bill dedicated the work of Yahweh here. During some of Bill's sermons later it was stated that the first sanctuary in the wilderness was "mobile," as was this sanctuary.

During this service I and another woman were ordained as Deaconess. Jacob and Bill anointed and laid hands on us for this office.

Jacob brought several copies of the December, 1980, issue of *The Prophetic Watchman*, his magazine, to pass out during his visit. Jacob and Bill were now working together, but this was not to last for very long.

CHAPTER EIGHT

1981
A House Divided

Bill's first booklet, *Give Me That Old Time Religion,* was published in Jacob's magazine, *The Prophetic Watchman,* in the January, 1981, edition beginning on page 20. The February, 1981, issue advertised the booklets that Bill had written, but nothing Bill had written was published. There was no magazine published by Jacob in March. In the next issue, April, 1981, Bill his booklets were not mentioned at all.

Bill had instigated a "cause" in order to separate himself from Jacob.

Previously, Bill had written numerous letters to Jacob questioning the customs of not mixing meat and milk in the same meal, of not eating beans and rice during Passover, and the necessity for men to grow beards.

Jacob would write very nice letters of rebuttal, trying to influence Bill to accept these teachings. On February 4, 1981, Bill wrote Jacob the letter that stated he could not accept the teaching of not mixing meat and milk. Bill separated himself from his brother, who established The House of Yahweh in Israel, and who ordained him as an Elder in this organization.

Bill quickly received three letters from Odessa, Texas. These letters pleaded with him to reconsider and to keep his promises. Jacob's letter reminded Bill of his responsibility to submit to his authority in The House of Yahweh. His letter, dated 2/8, 1981, follows in its entirety,

Dear Bill:

I received your letter written February 4, 1981. I do not need to say, that this letter was very saddening to read of the attitude that you have taken toward me, and The House of Yahweh doctrine.

The one thing that I have always wanted, that you be by my side in this work. I told Isabel, the day that you called about casting "LOTS" to see if you should come into The House of Yahweh, that I hoped nothing would come about to tear us apart anymore.

Now you have took the attitude which not only tears us apart Spiritually in the work of Yahweh, but will not allow us to even visit as a family anymore. The same attitude which has tore me apart from Tex, Gene and Margaret.

I wonder Bill, if you ever stoped (sic) to think about the day that you cast "LOTS" about The House of Yahweh? The day you did this, and Yahweh told you through casting of lots, to become a part of The House of Yahweh, The House of Yahweh was teaching that milk and meat should not be eat (sic) together, and that such things as beans and rice should not be eaten at Passover. Yahweh knew what The House of Yahweh was teaching, yet He told you to become a part of it. WAS THERE ANYTHING IN THOSE LOTS, THAT YOU SHOULD COME IN AND CHANGE THE HOUSE OF YAHWEH DOCTRINE? WASN'T THE LOTS CAST THAT YOU BECOME A PART OF THE HOUSE OF YAHWEH?

In 1973 when Yahweh led me to start proclaiming the establishment of His House upon the mountains of Israel, Yahweh knew exactly what I believed and taught. If I was so weak and wrong and teaching lies as you have accused me of doing, why did Yahweh choose me to lead His House? He knew where you were at that time and yes even where W. M. was. So why didn't He get you and W.M. to do this, as you two claim to be so right and I am such a liar? You had better stop and think of where you are standing!

Now concerning these "little ones" that you accuse me of turning away. I don't know who that they could be. You also say that the reason people have come to the Feasts and never came back was because we taught meat and milk should not be eaten together. THERE HAS NEVER BEEN ONE PERSON WHO LEFT THE HOUSE OF YAHWEH BECAUSE OF THE SUBJECT OF MEAT AND MILK. NOT EVEN W.– THE REASON W. DID NOT COME BACK, IS BECAUSE I TOLD HIM NOT TO COME BACK, UNTIL HE LEARNED TO RESPECT ME AS YAHWEH (sic) MINISTER. SO HE CALLED LAST FALL AND SAID THAT IF I WOULD LET HIM COME, HE WOULD NOT CAUSE ANY TROUBLE. BUT HE DID NOT KEEP HIS WORD.

I have never told you what I am going to tell you now, and would not be telling you now, if you had not of accused me of turning people away because of weakness. I did not want to hurt your feelings, though you have no respect for mine.

But the reason or the start of the reason for C.M. leaving The House of Yahweh, is because I stood up for you against him, when he was offended because you came to The House of Yahweh with two women. No meat and milk was involved in this at all.

The start of G.R. becoming upset with me, was the day you got up and brought that rigmarow (sic) about that 666. G. got mad that day and would not even stay to eat or talk to any one. He told me afterward that if I kept letting people get up and speak against The House of Yahweh doctrine and bring in false doctrine, that he was going to stop coming. All of this I am telling you, I can prove.

Also your (sic) not wearing a beard was a great offence (sic) to many. I was jumped on to by three or four people for ordaining you before you grew a beard. But I stood up for you and told them to give you time to grow into these things. Some of them still hold this against me. But instead of you taking an humble attitude, it looks as though you set in to discredet (sic) me in front of all in The House of Yahweh and prove to them that I am a false Prophet and that you came in to liberate the poor dumb members of The House of Yahweh.

I want to correct another thing. No one has said or taught that milk is blood or that it is unclean. But if you deny that it is made from a substance in the blood of the Mother, you deny a proven fact. If you deny that is (sic) is the very life of a baby, you deny another proven fact.

You say there is not Scripture that says you are not to eat milk and meat together. I say that there is, Deut. 14/21 which is given right here in the food law. I also say that you nor anyone else have any Scripture that says that you can eat milk and meat together. You know and I know that Gen. 18/1,8 does not say that the angels eat meat and milk together. Because we know how long it takes to dress and cook a whole calf. It took over a day last fall to cook that goat and then it had to be finished in the stove. I did not see any women in a hurry to make bread, when the goat was put in the pit. If Sarah was that slow in making bread, after being told to hurry, she sure was a slow woman.

Now, I don't care if no other person on this earth stands up for the truth, I will still hold to it, if all men forsake me. Paul said all men forsook him, 2 Tim. 1/15, they all forsook Yahshua and left Him to die. I guess I am no better than they. The sad part is the ones doing the forsaking will be lost. (Signed) Jacob

Jacob added a post-script with his letter, stating,

Bill, what kind of an example do you think you are setting in front of (Jacob's son-in-law)? All his life he has been taught that Yahshua was a false Messiah. He never heard the truth till he married (Jacob's daughter). Now as he is hearing and believing that Yahshua might be the Messiah, here comes people who trys (sic) to tear down the laws that he has been taught all of his life and were taught to his forefathers and which he reads in his own Hebrew Bible. That brings back the same old memory that has been taught to him and all Jews, that Yahshua could not be the Messiah because His followers try to abolish the laws of Yahweh which He gave to Moses for all Israel.

Jacob's youngest son reminded Bill that if he left The House of Yahweh that he would also lose his salvation, since he was also rebelling against the government of Yahweh. Excerpts from his letter follow,

Dear Bill

Shalom. Daddy received a letter from you dated February the 4. It was a very sad letter because we all love you and your family here. And we don't want to see you get out of the House of Yahweh.

Bill Yahshua came into this world for one purpose, and that was to save the people in His body...So Bill it stands to prove that if we are not in His Body we will not be saved.

Bill I know that you know the Bible well enough to know that there is only one body. For Yahshua only has one physical body, so then He would have only one spiritual body...Then Bill if there is only one body, there would be only one name in which the body of Messiah would be call. (sic)...And that name is the House of Yahweh. For Yahshua's body is the call (sic) out of this world...And Paul stated that the call (sic) out of the living Elohim is the House of Yahweh...So Bill this means that if you are not in the House of Yahweh you will not be saved, for Yahshua came only to save those in the House of Yahweh, His body.

This is why Bill your letter was very sad to us here. Because we don't want to see you lose your salvation or your familys' (sic).

Bill when we went to Israel we did not know why we were going there. O we thought we did, but we did not. Yahweh was leading Daddy there to start the House of Yahweh in the last days as the prophets fortold (sic). For Daddy had no attentions (sic) to start a House of Yahweh, you know that. But Yahweh lead (sic) him to.

Bill it was also fortold (sic) by the prophet Ezekiel. For he wrote that Yahweh would bring His people into the wilderness of the Gentiles, and there He would teach them the laws. And also here He would purge out the rebels, the ones that rebel against the government of Yahweh's House...

Bill...do you consider yourself one of the rebels and

transgresser (sic)? Bill they are the only ones that Yahweh is purging out of His House…

Bill the reason I am telling you this is because so that you can see that Yahweh has been leading Daddy to establish his House and to seal his people in the forheads (sic) before the great tribulation…And Daddy has been trying with all his heart to teach the laws and the name of Yahweh and Yahshua unto all the world…Then when you were ordain (sic) a Minister in the House of Yahweh. Daddy was very glad because he thought he would have you also to help teach the Evangel to all the world as Yahshua left command.

So Bill when you wrote that letter it hurt us all here very much, but it hurt Daddy and Momma the most. Because it seems you are relinquishing all family ties also. So it is very sad unto us all because we love you all there as family. and (sic) also as brother and sisters in the faith of Yahshua, which Yahweh led Daddy to establish again in these last days.

Bill I hope that you will reconsider because your SALVATION is at stake. May Yahweh bless you to reconsider. Shalom in Yahshua's name, (signed) Jacob's son

Jacob's wife reminded Bill that he knew the doctrine of The House of Yahweh when he was ordained. In her letter dated Feb 8-81, she wrote,

Bill

I feel I need to write you at this time regarding your letter written Feb 4. Your letter was a very nasty one. I cannot see how the Holy Spirit could lead anyone to write such a letter…

Bill you know that you left Yahweh and the ministry years ago to seek your material wants. Jacob stayed with the ministry enduring hardships to teach the truth. Now years later you come up saying Yahweh sent you to warn Jacob. Heaven knows I tried. as (sic) you stated. My, my how ignorant can one become. Yahweh has been very nice to you because He has given you another opportunity to get salvation. but (sic) unless you give up that pride and become humble and to understand that you don't know it all. Yahweh then will be able to use you.

Bill you are blessed with a talent to make money and use it wisely. But you need a leader where the Bible is concerned. Jacob never was blessed with wealth but he was blessed teaching the Bible. You know this for how many times have you called up asking him to explain the scriptures to you. You even told some one that last Sabbath you were here that Jacob taught you everything you know about the Bible.

Bill the only step you took when you came out of Armstrong is teaching the name. You are teaching every thing else Armstrong teaches. You knew the doctron (sic) of the House of Yahweh when you came into it, so for the love of Yahweh what is your trouble?

...This may come as a surprise to both you and Kay. But you and Kay are the only ones here that ever left the House of Yahweh over this subject of meat and milk...

Bill this is the third time Yahweh has given you a (sic) opportunity to help Jacob teach the truth. Please don't blow it this time...

I pray you will let Yahweh lead you in this, before you really make a stand. Love to all, (signed) Isabel

Each of their letters pointed out the fact that Bill was not submitting to the authority placed over him. Bill has no problem with authority. He wants to "be the authority"—not submit to it.

It is ironic that years later he would be hammering "submission to authority" to the congregation of The House of Yahweh, Abilene—when years earlier he refused to submit to the same authority which was placed over him in The House of Yahweh, Odessa.

By the time Bill's letter was written on February 4, 1981, Bill had already made up his mind—therefore, his "cause" to separate himself from Jacob Hawkins.

Bill lost no time consulting with Attorney Dan Abbott to file for "House of Yahweh, Texas Charter No. 554949," and indicated on the Application that the date incorporated or formed was on March 19, 1981.

There was no way that Bill was going to be under the authority of Jacob Hawkins, or anyone else.

Another young Elder in the Odessa congregation wrote another letter to Bill, post-marked March 10, 1981. The excerpts from his letter state,

> Dear Bill,
>
> Hi. Received your last letter…I was hoping that your last letter at least showed that you're not closed to further discussion.
>
> You remember in my last letter I talked about the incident of the Apostles & Elders meeting with James the overseer of The House of Yahweh to discuss the question of circumcision and what to do with the gentiles.
>
> You know if Kepha would have not agreed with James' decision and thought gentiles shouldn't have to do what James said and would have left off working with him and continued to preach on his own, according to Saul he would have been accursed. Galatians 1:8-9. Or if Saul would have not gone along with it and would have said, "I'll still pray for your work but I'm not going to be a part of it," according to himself (Galatians 1:8-9) he would be accursed.
>
> Either a person gathers with Yahshua or scatters abroad, one sheepfold. There's only ONE House of Yahweh. It started in Nazareth, Israel, Yahshua's hometown.
>
> Now, Bill I hope you carefully consider this, Yahshua prayed for unity among His people. Saul said to "all speak the same thing and that there be no divisions among you; but that ye be perfectly joined together in the same judgement." I Cor. 1:10.
>
> Bill, we need to strive…for unity, not division. It might be better if you came down here, brought your books, and we discuss this reasonably and rationally and come to a conclusion.
>
> Bill Jacob found some more information on this subject of meat and milk at the library. I hope you don't read this going in with the attitude of pre-disagreement and trying to tear it apart without giving yourself an opportunity to understand the truth of the matter.
>
> Bill, I'm hoping you'll take this to heart the way Yahweh wants to with the attitude pleasing to Him…if we didn't love you like we do down here we wouldn't be trying so hard to

prevent a split between us... Still hoping and praying. (Signed) JR

Although Bill wanted to separate from Jacob and his organization, Bill did not want to completely separate himself from Jacob and his literature. It would have been very difficult, if not impossible, over the years for Bill to have topics ready for publication in *The Prophetic Word* magazine without the articles already published in *The Prophetic Watchman* magazine. Since Jacob never copyrighted his work, Bill felt free to steal his writings, ideas, phrases, and the name "House of Yahweh."

There were now two organizations named "The House of Yahweh." One was in Odessa, Texas, led by Elder and Overseer Jacob Hawkins, established on the mountains of Israel and brought back to the United States. The other organization was in Eula, Texas, led by Elder and Overseer Bill Hawkins. The weekly Sabbaths and Feasts of Passover and Unleavened Bread, Pentecost, and the Feast of Tabernacles were celebrated in the "mobile sanctuary" in Eula in 1981, but Bill wanted bigger and better. So he set out to build The House of Yahweh in the city of Abilene, Texas.

Bill wrote another, rather gloating and insensitive, letter to Jacob, dated September 23, 1981, stating,

> Greeting in Yahshua's Name,
> ...Thank you for sending the correspondence course...
> The House of Yahweh is growing here in Abilene. We have outgrown the Mobile Home and are now building a large Sanctuary on the 10 ½ acres on T&P Lane in Abilene. We are all rejoicing.
>
> I keep telling the congregation here about the House of Yahweh in Odessa. They are all most anxious to meet all of you.
>
> Jacob, I wish for the sake of Yahweh's Work we could all work together. If you have thought of anyway we could reconcile this matter I would like to hear from you.
>
> I know Yahweh will bring us together eventually but I would like that it could be now...Matthew 5:23,24. Love in Yahshua's Name, (signed) Bill Hawkins

Jacob immediately responded to Bill's remark about reconciliation. Excerpts from Jacob's letter dated 9/24, 1981, state,

...Now about us getting back together and working together. We can do this if you agree to these rules.

1.   That The House of Yahweh in Odessa is the headquarters of all Houses of Yahweh that will be raised up in the world.

2.   That all doctrine is to be settled in Odessa by the Overseer, just as is commanded in the Law of Yahweh and was done during the days of the Apostles...

3.   That when a decision is made by the Overseer concerning a doctrine, that doctrine is to be accepted as binding by all Ministers of The House of Yahweh, and they are to teach it to the congregations.

4.   That Pastors of local congregations are to pay into The House of Yahweh headquarters in Odessa, 10% of all tithe which they receive and have as commanded in the Law...

5.   That all converts made by any Pastor or Minister be taught that they must keep the three feasts Passover, Pentecost, and Feast of Tabernacles at The House of Yahweh headquarters in Odessa as commanded in the Law...

6.   That The Prophetic Watchman is the official magazine of The House of Yahweh, and all literature printed must be approved by the headquarters in Odessa.

Now what I have written here is according to the Law of Yahweh, and is what the Law teaches. I do not see why we can't work together this way... (Signed) Jacob

Bill did not comply with these rules. Instead, Bill wrote another letter in rebuttal to Jacob, dated September 24, 1981, stating that there was no "Law" against mixing meat and milk in all the Holy Scriptures, and that the word "eat" is not written in Exodus 23:9, Exodus 34:26, and

Deuteronomy 14:21. <u>Bill accused Jacob of accepting "interpretations of men" rather than allowing Scripture to interpret the Scripture.</u>

Bill accused Jacob of trying to set himself up as the pope, the only one in authority who had power over all the others. Bill went on to state,

> ...whosoever will be great among you, let him be your minister...whosoever will be chief among you, let him be your servant:
> The House of Yahweh would have a very unstable foundation if established on a <u>fallible human being</u>...
> It should frighten you to teach such doctrines as they taught, Jacob. I would work with you from now on the spread the Inspired Scriptures, but don't ask me to <u>spread interpretations of men who shut up the Kingdom of Heaven by twisting and changing Yahweh's Word</u>...I don't see why we can't work together spreading Yahweh's word <u>without</u> teaching the <u>interpretations of men</u>...
> The only thing that has caused people to turn away are (sic) THOSE INTERPRETATIONS...not the Inspired Scripture. Love in Yahshua's Name, (signed) Bill

It is ironic that Bill Hawkins once chastised Jacob Hawkins for promoting the government of Yahweh led by only one man, and for spreading interpretations of men through the twisting of scriptures. Yisrayl Bill Hawkins is now guilty of committing both sins.

Pioneers of The Church of God, Seventh Day, in the early 1930s, Andrew N. Dugger and C.O. Dodd, set up their church government based upon the spiritual organization of the Twelve, the Seven, and the Seventy,

- The Twelve to look after the spiritual affairs of the church,
- The Seven to take charge of the financial business, and
- The Seventy to go forth two by two in giving the warning message for the hour. [26]

---

26 *A History of The True Church, Traced from 33 A.D. to Date,* Copyright 1936 by A.N. Dugger and C.O. Dodd for *The Bible Advocate,* Salem, W.VA, USA, page 299.

It is noteworthy here that both Jacob Hawkins and Bill Hawkins studied under Andrew N. Dugger at Midwest Bible College in Stanberry, Missouri, in 1957. Jacob and Bill should have been aware of the form of "church government" taught by The Church of God, Seventh Day—the government of "many"—not of only "one."

Herbert W. Armstrong was ordained as an Elder in The Church of God, Seventh Day, under the leadership of Andrew. N. Dugger. Herbert W. Armstrong was then chosen to become one of The Seventy on November 4, 1933, in Salem, West Virginia.[27]

Herbert W. Armstrong was fully aware of this form of church government, but did not remain true to it, He eventually proclaimed himself to be "God's Only Apostle."

Jacob Hawkins and Buffalo Bill Hawkins did not follow this pattern either. Each of these men set up their own government of "one"—like kings ruling over a kingdom, holding absolute power and authority.

Jacob was proclaimed to be the "One Prophet." Yisrayl Bill Hawkins is proclaimed to be the "Anointed One."

The kingdoms of Herbert W. Armstrong and of Jacob Hawkins: The Worldwide Church of God and The House of Yahweh, Odessa—have now been overthrown.

Only Buffalo Bill Hawkins' kingdom, The House of Yahweh, Abilene, ruled over by Yisrayl Bill Hawkins, remains as of this writing. It is now only a matter of time before his kingdom, also, will be no more.

---

27 *A History of The True Church,* Dugger and Dodd, pages 303-304.

CHAPTER NINE

1981-1983
Building the Structure in Abilene

The ten and one-half acres that Bill and I had purchased in 1974, was the place to begin to grow the work of The House of Yahweh in Abilene, Texas. The City of Abilene issued the permit to build. The main sanctuary, with classrooms and a kitchen area, was started in September, 1981, with the setting of plumbing and the pouring of the concrete slab by outside contractors. Through the very warm fall months of 1981, Bill and the construction crew set the walls and roof joists, hung doors and windows, installed the roofing, and one of the members, Walter Jandrisevits, did the brickwork. A baptism tank was constructed from fiberglass and positioned in an area behind the pulpit; the bathroom plumbing was roughed in as was the electrical. The insulation was installed, and the sheetrock was hung by the end of November.

The first celebration in The House of Yahweh, Abilene, was The Feast of Dedication-Chanukkah, on December 21, 1981. At this time the structure was dedicated. A children's play about the Feast of Dedication was presented, and a wonderful party was celebrated afterward. Everyone had a great time.

The finish work in the main sanctuary continued into 1982; walls were textured and painted, flooring and carpeting was laid, new pews were set and my childhood piano was moved from the Mobile Sanctuary in Eula to Abilene. The central air conditioning was wonderful.

Incorporation of The House of Yahweh

Bill then set out to legally establish The House of Yahweh, Abilene, by forming a corporation to obtain exemption from Federal Income Tax by the Internal Revenue Service. On February 5, 1982, Attorney Dan Abbott filed documents with the District Director, Internal Revenue Service, in Dallas, Texas, for House of Yahweh, Texas Charter No. 554949, date incorporated or formed, March 19, 1981. Our Articles of Incorporation listed Bill Hawkins as President, Kay Hawkins as Secretary, and Dennis Hawkins as Treasurer.

Bill preached the first sermon around the end of February, 1982, that the men should wear a "kippah" on their heads in reverence for Yahweh. All of the women in the congregation were already wearing head coverings during services, but not all the men were doing so. Some of the men did not think this was necessary. The men who did not think that wearing a kippah was necessary, and their families, left the congregation. This was our first trial and it was bitterly painful.

The Name Change and The Two Witnesses

About this same time Bill again began to think about the name given to him at birth, and decided that it was time to change it. We had been studying the name of "Israel," and had come to the understanding that the suffix, "el," referred to the word for "god." Bill did not want to be named after a god, so the "el" suffix was changed to the "yl" suffix, which signified the word, "power."

The word, *Israel,* in *Strong's Exhaustive Concordance, Hebrew Dictionary,* word #3478,[4] is written as *Yisrael.* Bill chose the name, "Yisrayl."

On March 16, 1982, Buffalo Bill Hawkins' name was legally changed to Yisrayl Bill Hawkins in Cause No. 6998-C, also filed by Attorney Dan Abbott.

At first Yisrayl signed his name, Yisrayl B. Hawkins. When it was pointed out to him that "Yisrayl B" calculated to the number 666, which is the mark of the beast, Yisrayl started signing his name simply, Yisrayl Hawkins.

There was also another reason for changing his name to Yisrayl; he could become one of The Two Witnesses mentioned in Isaiah Chapter 44.

I remember the time that Yisrayl, very shortly after his name was legally changed, showed this scripture to me from the Holy Name Bible, written in Isaiah 44:7 in this version,[5] which states,

> One shall say, I am Yahweh's; and another shall call himself by the name of Jacob; and another shall subscribe with his hand unto Yahweh, and surname himself by the name of Israel.

I was overcome with emotion and joy. This would validate both organizations of The House of Yahweh. Yes, Jacob and Yisrayl would both work together some day. Yisrayl quickly composed a sermon to bring this revelation to the congregation; the rationale for being "The Two Witnesses" written in the scriptures.

The booklet entitled, *The Two Witnesses,* was first printed in June, 1983, and became the published rationale for the work of The House of Yahweh, under Jacob and Yisrayl, in the Last Days.

The Passover and Feast of Unleavened Bread in the spring of 1982 was the first scriptural feast celebrated in The House of Yahweh, Abilene. Four tables were set up in the dining room, which seated about twenty-two people who observed the Passover. The Feast of Unleavened Bread continued for seven days, with preaching on the Sabbaths and High Days only. The members did not camp on the grounds this first feast, but the children were excused from school.

The building work continued with the setting of the sidewalks and paving the parking lot. The Feast of Pentecost was celebrated in May.

The Prophetic Word

We started purchasing copies of the *Holy Name Bible* around 1978, when Jacob introduced us to this translation. We found the scripture in Jeremiah 23:36, which stated,

> ...For the message cometh unto man, by the prophetic word...[6]

The title was perfect. The very first magazine, published by The

House of Yahweh, Abilene, in September, 1982, was called *The Prophetic Word*.

Our first advertisement about the Name of the Creator was also published in the classified ads in the *National Enquirer* [7] in 1982. Magazines, letters and sermon tapes began to be sent throughout the United States. The Mailing List steadily grew and so did the expense for sending these items first class postage. We were waiting patiently for The House of Yahweh organization to be declared exempt from Federal Income Tax as a non-profit religious organization. We would then receive special postage rates.

Non-Profit 501(c)(3) Status

On September 30, 1982, The House of Yahweh was incorporated as a Non-Profit organization by the State of Texas, but it would not be until February 4, 1983, that The House of Yahweh was determined to be exempt from Federal Income Tax under section 501(c)(3) of the Internal Revenue Code.

On February 11, 1983, we filed with the United States Postal Service for Non-Profit Religious postal rates. Through this determination it was also our opinion that it was the action of "incorporation" that "established" The House of Yahweh in Abilene, Texas.

CHAPTER TEN

My Son and The Yliyah School

On August 31, 1983, my son Dennis turned seventeen-years-old. That morning he said bye to me and then he and a friend ran away from home. They hitchhiked to Weatherford, Texas, about one hundred miles away, before the sheriff found them and called the house. I had been frantic with worry about them. The other boy returned to his home but Dennis had called me and told me he was not coming back to the abuse that he had been suffering. I then remembered the day that Dennis had turned sixteen.

I had baked a cake for him, which we shared at the evening meal. There were no parties or gifts in celebration of birthdays, but the family could have private acknowledgments. The next morning, Yisrayl took the cake and threw it, pan and all, out the back door. Dennis found it, broken and scattered, when he walked out to go milk the cows. I remembered the look of pain on his face when he told me. I felt anguish and sorrow for him. I felt hatred and anger toward Yisrayl Hawkins. How could a man do that to his son?

I had felt helpless to do anything about it at that time. I thought about what I could do for Dennis now.

Yisrayl came in later and said he was driving to Weatherford to pick Dennis up. I told him that Dennis was not coming home, and would not have to come home since he was seventeen and could decide for himself. I had already called my dad in Royston and asked him to go get Dennis, which he did. Yisrayl did not know that I had already done this. He would never have accepted responsibility for driving Dennis away from home, which he most certainly did, and then he would have become even more abusive than ever. I wanted to save Dennis from this.

Yisrayl did the same thing to my middle son, David, at about the same age, when he moved David out of our home into Abilene to live next to his sister. Dena's son suffered this same rejection at age sixteen. I understand now that Yisrayl Hawkins expects the young men in his organization to move out of their homes, away from their mothers. They are the equivalent of the "lost boys" in the fundamentalist Mormon homes where polygamy is also practiced—some more of the "fruit" by which you will know him.

With Dennis gone there was no one at home to milk the cows and do all the other farm work, so this burden now started to fall on our other children. The farm buildings and the outside of my home also began to slowly dilapidate.

Yisrayl did not have Dennis' help during the summer of 1984, so therefore he had more responsibilities at our mobile home park in Abilene. Yisrayl, true to form, began to grow bored with maintaining and being responsible for this business. The mobile homes also slowly began to dilapidate even more, and the whole place began to look worse than a seedy, run-down dump.

In July, 1984, we began the process of selling out. The land was rezoned. Yisrayl was advised by our real estate agent to move the mobile homes onto our land at T&P Lane in order to methodically sell these at a fair price. He didn't take this sound advice. Instead, Yisrayl obtained the services of an auctioneer, but negotiated with him for a flat fee for the sale, rather than a percentage of the proceeds. Yisrayl thought he was saving money. What a mistake that was.

When the auction began, I couldn't believe how fast and cheap these trailers were being auctioned off, which included Yisrayl's office at the park. Yisrayl did not know that he could have set reservations for a minimum price, because the auctioneer did not feel obliged to let him know—he was not being paid for any other services, including advice. We barely received enough to pay off the land cost. By September 17, all that remained was a scraped-clean lot.

On November 1, 1984, we sold this land, but possession would eventually return to us due to the Texas oil bust depression which occurred shortly afterward. With the large down payment we received at closing, we paid off the lands that we had purchased, which included the ten and one-half acres on T&P Lane. We would eventually sell this property on South Treadaway, but Yisrayl Hawkins would have total control of every penny of the proceeds.

Of course, it was not Yisrayl's fault that Dennis had "rebelled" against him; this wasn't his fault. He blamed the Eula Public School System. Our other children began to be "home schooled" in the fall of 1984. They indicated that they hated it.

The Yliyah School was established afterward. Classes were then held in Abilene. Eventually two brick veneer school buildings would be built on our private property on Highway 603 in Eula. Most of the children attending The House of Yahweh during this time were educated here. I would become a member of the school board. Textbooks were purchased from the Texas School Depository, and the children followed the same curricula as that of the public schools. We also dismissed school when the feasts were celebrated.

My first grandchild was being educated at this same school in 1994, the year that I was excommunicated. I would not be allowed to attend her end-of-school graduation and promotion parties and festivities. I had never missed one of these functions before. I felt sadness and regret.

CHAPTER ELEVEN

1985-1991
The Book of Yahweh and
The Trademark Battle

In 1985 we began to work on our own translation of the bible using the correct names. We had come to an understanding that the majority of the words in the bible ending in "el" referred to the word "god." At first, many of us would meet in the sanctuary dining hall in Abilene, be given a copy of a page from the *Holy Name Bible*,[8] and literally paste the letter, "y" over the letter, "e," in words like Isra(y)l, Dani(y)l, and Ang(y)l.

We thought we would be able to do this and print our own bibles. The more we researched, the more changes would have to be made, and it was not just to change the letter "e" to the letter "y."

In March,1986, we purchased a used typesetting machine, and for the next year I would be focused on typesetting this new version of the bible. We did not know the name for our translation until much later. The Prophet Isaiah (Isayah) revealed it to us, in Isayah 34:16—*The Book of Yahweh.*

The First Printing of *The Book of Yahweh*[9] was published on October 30, 1987, and the copyright was registered November 3. The first edition of this bible was noted as editing, annotations, name restoration and rephrasing into modern English. Lubbock, Texas, Attorney Wendell Coffee assisted in the copyright registration.

The Second Printing of *The Book of Yahweh*[10] was published on September 21, 1988, and was also a work of editing, annotations, name restoration and rephrasing into modern English, mainly correcting typographical errors.

Again, Mr. Coffee assisted in its copyright registration. I was personally involved with these first two editions. The name of the author on the First Edition of the copyright document is, The House of Yahweh, a non-profit corporation of the State of Texas, Employer of Yisrayl Hawkins. The author on the Second Edition is Yisrayl Hawkins.

I have copies of both of these editions. Yisrayl Hawkins personally autographed my copy of The Book of Yahweh, Second Printing, stating,

> To my one and only 9-28-88 Mrs. Kay Hawkins from Yisrayl Hawkins. May this help you always to serve our Creator & Friend, Yahweh of host.

At this time, I was his "one and only."

In the process of getting *The Book of Yahweh* officially copyrighted the first time, Yisrayl discussed the possibility of obtaining a "Trademark" for The House of Yahweh organization. We learned that the "organization" itself could not be trademarked. We were advised by Mr. Coffee how to proceed.

Beginning about this time the books and booklets published began to bear the "brand," *A House of Yahweh Publication.*

We were advised that we could "Trademark" this when we could prove that our printed material was branded in this way. The 1988 Edition, Second Printing, of *The Book of Yahweh* has this notation. Yisrayl again contacted Wendell Coffee about registering The House of Yahweh brand as a trademark or service mark.

On December 5, 1988, Yisrayl signed the application. Wendell Coffee filed the document on December 19 to register the Trademark, "HOUSE OF YAHWEH" in the United States. A search had been made, and there was no name on record that "HOUSE OF YAHWEH" was being used as a Trademark—we were the first.

On June 19, 1989, we received a letter from Mr. Coffee stating that he had received notice from the Patent and Trademark Office that our mark would be published for opposition in the July 4, 1989, edition of the Official Gazette, and that if no one opposed or contested our right to register this mark, a registration would issue about three months after publication. Everything was going according to schedule.

The tentative trademark, "HOUSE OF YAHWEH," was published on July 4, 1989. Then the hammer suddenly fell upon us. We learned that Jacob O. Meyer, Elder and Overseer of the Assemblies of Yahweh in Bethel, PA., was opposing our Trademark Application for HOUSE OF YAHWEH!

It was in 1985 that we first heard that this sacred name group had filed a lawsuit against another sacred name group, and they had reached an agreement about, among other things, infringement of their organizational name.

Jacob O. Meyer sent this letter to the people on his mailing list, dated June 11, 1985. Excerpts from this letter follow,

> To whom this may concern…An out of court settlement has been reached in the lawsuit brought by Assemblies of Yahweh against the Rocheport, Missouri, group which had been operating under the name "Assemblies of Yahweh in Messiah."…We are advised that the leaders of the Rocheport group have set out some of the features of the settlement in a recent letter to their members. Some of you may have seen that letter. For the benefit of those who have not learned of the settlement terms, we can advise that the agreement calls for the Rocheport group to change its name, to pay $20,000 in damages to the Assemblies of Yahweh in installments over the next year, for injuries to Assemblies of Yahweh as a result of infringement of the organizational name and misappropriation of mailing lists, and to pay the court costs in the case. The settlement agreement expressly approves their use of the new name "Yahweh's Assembly in Messiah," but rightfully assigns to us their previous name "Assemblies of Yahweh in Messiah."

The letter of opposition came from William H. Elliott, Jr., with the Law Offices of Synnestvedt & Lechner in Philadelphia, Pennsylvania, and is dated September 19, 1989. Yisrayl brought this letter to me and I became terrified. To me, this meant that Meyer wanted to destroy The

House of Yahweh, since he had already come against other sacred name groups about their organizational names. This letter states,

Dear Mr. Coffee:

In line with our phone discussion today, I would be prepared to recommend to my clients that they agree to refrain from opposing the above application and not object to your client's use of the term HOUSE OF YAHWEH for religious printed publications, provided your client would undertake and agree as follows:

1. Withdraw application Serial No. 73/769813

2. Agree not to refile the application for religious printed publications or for goods or services of any kind of a religious nature.

3. Cancel any state, trade or service mark registrations that they or Yisrael Hawkins may have obtained for "HOUSE OF YAHWEH" or composites thereof.

4. Refrain from objecting to my client's generic use of the term "House of Yahweh" in its publications, a frequent usage when referring to the Temple.

I look forward to hearing from you regarding this proposal. Yours very truly, signed William H. Elliott, Jr.

When Mr. Coffee sent this letter to us, he stated in his own letter,

...As you may see from his letter, he is offering no compromise. He is offering to settle it where he would get more than he would if he were to win the opposition.

Obviously I do not recommend that we accept the offer of his client.

You might consider that you would make a counter-offer that you would refrain from objecting to any generic use of Jacob Meyer's of the term, "House of Yahweh." However, I would certainly recommend not agreeing either to any of the other three...

The battle line was drawn to save The House of Yahweh from being swallowed up by Jacob O. Meyer and his organization. This war of words and letters became my responsibility. I was determined that The House of Yahweh would not be destroyed by this.

Yisrayl would receive the letters in Abilene. He would then turn them over to me to compose the lists, documents, proof, etc. When the work was completed, all Yisrayl had to do was sign his name.

This responsibility was added to my regular responsibilities for the entire duration of this ordeal.

The Patent and Trademark office received Jacob Meyer's Opposition on November 6, 1989. The correspondence was deposited with the US Postal Service on November 2, addressed to: Commissioner of Patents and Trademarks, Washington, D.C. 20231, In the matter of Trademark application Serial No. 73/769,813 published in the Official Gazette on July 4, 1989.

Assemblies of Yahweh, Opposer v. The House of Yahweh, Applicant
Opposition No. 81476.

There were eight grounds listed in opposition of our application. Ground No. 8 specifically stated that our registration would likely cause confusion or deception or mistake about Meyer's Trademark, Service Mark, "ASSEMBLIES OF YAHWEH," and it and the public would be damaged.

At this time we discovered that Meyer had been issued Trademark, Service Mark Reg. No. 1,508,075 on October 11, 1988.

Wendell Coffee sent 16 pages of The House of Yahweh's First Set of Interrogatories to Assemblies of Yahweh on May 11, 1990. On June 6, Meyer proposed an agreement between Assemblies of Yahweh and House of Yahweh, which we refused.

On June 18, 1990, Mr. Coffee sent us a letter, along with 36 pages of the Opposers' Discovery Requests:

Part I. Opposer's First Set of Interrogatories to Applicant.
Part II. Opposer's First Set of Requests for Production of Documents.
Part III. Opposer's First Set of Requests for Admissions.

Included with Meyer's documents was a copy of *The Prophetic*

Watchman magazine, published by Jacob Hawkins, Vol.1 No.11, August, 1973, in which Jacob publishes the name, *The House of Yahweh,* for the very first time.

Now we knew that Meyer was using the strategy that Jacob Hawkins was the original recipient of the organizational name, "HOUSE OF YAHWEH," and we learned that Meyer had contacted Jacob about it. We were advised that the deadline for Meyer's attorney to receive all this information was July 12, 1990, just one month later. I thought to myself, "There is no way that I can respond to Meyer's Discovery Requests in just one month."

We changed attorneys on July 10, 1990. H. Bryce Parker III resided in Abilene and it was more convenient to receive personal attention to this vital matter. We applied for and received an extension of the July 12, 1990, deadline to submit our answers to Meyer, until August 12, 1990—giving me more time to respond.

During one of our brainstorms with Bryce, it was decided that we would contact Jacob Hawkins in Odessa, and ask him if he would join with The House of Yahweh, Abilene, in the lawsuit against Jacob O. Meyer and his Assemblies of Yahweh. We would Authorize and License each other.

This was the last time that Jacob and Yisrayl worked together. On July 4, 1990, by Notary Public signature, Yisrayl Hawkins Authorized and Licensed Jacob-Yaaqob Hawkins and Jacob-Yaaqob Hawkins Authorized and Licensed Yisrayl Hawkins to protect the name, The House of Yahweh, from Jacob O. Meyer. These documents of Authorization and Licensure state,

> Know all men by these presents that I, Yisrayl Hawkins, AUTHORIZE AND LICENSE and have heretofore verbally authorized and licensed Jacob Hawkins, also known as Yaaqob Hawkins, to use the Name: THE HOUSE OF YAHWEH in any Religious Work, Organization, etc, as a Trade Name, Service Mark, etc. with the authority to copyright same in his OWN NAME, in perpetuity to himself his heirs or assigns. (Signed) Yisrayl Hawkins Elder & Overseer The House of Yahweh, Abilene, Texas."

Know all men by these presents that I, Jacob Hawkins, also

known as Yaaqob Hawkins, AUTHORIZE AND LICENSE and have heretofore verbally authorized and licensed Yisrayl Hawkins, to use the Name: THE HOUSE OF YAHWEH in any Religious Work, Organization, etc, as a Trade Name, Service Mark, etc. with the authority to copyright same in his OWN NAME, in perpetuity to himself his heirs or assigns.
(Signed) Jacob Hawkins, Yaaqob Hawkins
The House of Yahweh, Odessa, Texas

On August 3, 1990, H. Bryce Parker III sent 92 pages of our Applicants' Answers to Opposer's Discovery Requests to William H. Elliott, Meyer's attorney. In this documentation Jacob O. Meyer was informed that,

1. Yaaqob (Jacob) and Yisrayl Hawkins and no others led The House of Yahweh; that

2. The organizations originated in the USA and Israel.

3. We are and will always be the House of Yahweh and there are no others, and

4. Authorize and License each other to use and protect the name, the House of Yahweh.

Regretfully, before Jacob O. Meyer's attorney could respond, our attorney, H. Bryce Parker III, died by apparent suicide. We were first informed of his death by *The Abilene Reporter News.* We would have to get another attorney, and fast.

I frantically called the Lawyer Referral number and thereafter I contacted Glaser, Griggs & Schwartz, Attorneys at Law in Dallas, Texas, who specialized in Patent, Trademark, Copyright & Related Matters. Attorney W. Kirk McCord agreed to accept our case.

In Mr. McCord's letter dated October 10, 1990, he requested that I send him a copy of our files to see what, if anything, might be missing from the file he received from Mr. Parker's office, which I did.

By October 16, 1990, W. Kirk McCord had prepared our Applicant's Supplemental Answers. By November 2, 1990, he was negotiating a Settlement with Jacob O. Meyer and the Assemblies of Yahweh.

The United States Department of Commerce, Patent and Trademark

Office, in a letter mailed to W. Kirk McCord on December 13, 1990, states:

> Opposer, without the written consent of applicant, filed a withdrawal of the opposition on November 19, 1990. Rule 2.106(c) provides that, after an answer is filed, the opposition may not be withdrawn without prejudice except with the written consent of applicant. In view thereof, and since the withdrawal was filed after answer, the opposition is dismissed with prejudice. Signed, R.L. Simms, E. W. Hanak, T.J. Quinn Members, Trademark Trial and Appeal Board.

On December 20, 1990, W. Kirk McCord sent this letter,

Dear Yisrayl:
Enclosed is a copy of the order of the Trademark Trial and Appeal Board, dismissing the subject opposition with prejudice. The fact that the opposition has been dismissed with prejudice means that the Opposer cannot refile the opposition against this particular registration. Assemblies of Yahweh is not precluded, however, from opposing any future applications for trademark registration which you may file... Very truly yours, W. Kirk McCord

We had won! There was no way that Jacob O. Meyer and his Assemblies of Yahweh could swallow us up now. He would not be able to stop the printing, publishing, and ministry of The House of Yahweh. I was so relieved and grateful for the victory that Yahweh had given to us.

It was not until April 16, 1991, that the United States Patent and Trademark Office issued the Certificate of Registration No. 1641225 as a Trademark, "HOUSE OF YAHWEH." It was a wonderful thing to see.

CHAPTER TWELVE

1984 -1990
The Beginning of The End
And The Golden Age

The first members of The House of Yahweh, Abilene, were initially people who lived in Abilene or who rented from us. From December, 1980, until the spring of 1984 this remained constant. It would not be until Passover of 1984 that seven people on our out of town mailing list responded to our invitation to attend one of Yahweh's feasts, and every individual who came was of African American descent!

This should come as no surprise to anyone, but Yisrayl Hawkins was a very bigoted, prejudiced man, so this was a true test. It was not unlike the prejudice of the first Apostles who considered the gentiles to be common and unclean. Yahweh had to work a miracle for the first gentile, Cornelius, to be accepted by them. So, Yahweh had called and sent seven people who would truly test his bigotry and prejudice.

There were seven new members baptized into The House of Yahweh on Sunday, April 15, 1984. Yahshua's Memorial was celebrated on April 15 at sunset, and the Feast of Passover and Days of Unleavened Bread began April 16 at sunset and continued through April 23 at sunset.

However, at first, just as Herbert W. Armstrong had done before him, Yisrayl Hawkins relegated the blacks in the congregation to a completely segregated area of the New World to Come. They would be set apart in a land all by themselves.

The growth of the membership between 1984 and 1986 was slow but steady. New people were coming to each of the feasts, and some of the most unique members arrived from Wisconsin on Pentecost, June 14, 1986. By the time the Feast of Tabernacles came around, we had learned about "food storage" in preparation for withstanding the Great Tribulation.

Yisrayl thought this was great. He set out to buy wheat and sell it for a profit to the people in the congregation, only he didn't let the people know this. They thought they were getting this at cost. He could have told them there would be extra charges, but he didn't. When he told me what he was going to do, I begged him not to do this. I told him this was not right, that this was deception, and that this was wrong. Again, he refused to listen to me.

To shorten a long story, a very intelligent woman, who did not trust Yisrayl Hawkins, contacted the establishment where the wheat was purchased and was informed about the correct, lower, price. When she confronted Yisrayl about this, rather than admit his guilt, apologize, and return the difference to everyone, he set out to discredit and destroy her. Remember, it is never his fault when anything goes wrong.

Elder Walter Jandrisevits, cunningly deceived and manipulated by Yisrayl, delivered the death blow during his sermon about heretics and those who fall away. She and her family left The House of Yahweh, Abilene, but they certainly did not leave The Faith. I am very sorry about this, and I pray that she accepts my apology. I would one day personally learn how it felt.

This was the first incident in The House of Yahweh where Yisrayl Hawkins tried to "make merchandise" of the members. From 1980 until 1986 he had behaved himself. I thought Yisrayl had actually repented and had turned from his old habits, but at this point I knew that he had not. I knew what Yisrayl had done. I was ashamed of him and angry at him. I had been through so much emotional turmoil up to this time because of his thoughtless, stupid antics. I didn't want to be a part of that anymore.

It was at this point that I slowly began to emotionally withdraw from Yisrayl Hawkins because of the pain, physical and emotional, that he inflicted. I started to draw very close to Yahweh, His Son, and my children, in this order.

Beginning with this incident, I began to focus on the spiritual work of Yahweh, and gladly accepted all responsibilities. I did not have to be around Yisrayl Hawkins to accomplish this. I left him to his own devices, and Yisrayl Hawkins began to surround himself with those who would agree with him about everything, without questioning anything.

The beginning of the end of the righteous work of Yahweh began here, when Yisrayl Hawkins began to think that he had the right to "make merchandise" out of the family members of The House of Yahweh.

Drawing Near to Satan

The year 1989 was when Yisrayl started thinking that he could "...cast out demons..." He read the scripture in Matthew 10:8, which, by his interpretation, gave him this authority. In fact, when Yisrayl Hawkins started thinking that he had this "authority," he was actually "usurping authority" which the Messiah had given to his Twelve Apostles, as Matthew 10:1 and 5 clearly state.

After this, Yisrayl Hawkins, and some of the Elders who surrounded him, believed that they had this power. There were actual instances in which this spectacle was taking place. DeeDee told me that she heard the voice of Satan during one of these events. Another report was that one of the men was actually lifted up and thrown against the wall as he was speaking to someone who was supposed to have been possessed.

The very first time that I heard about "casting out demons" was when I was sitting in the sanctuary in Abilene. This was on one of the New Moon meetings, and it was in the evening. Chills of fear ran through me. This was a dangerous practice. I do believe there is a spiritual world, and I believe that Satan is part of it. I had to drive home by myself. I felt movements under the driver's seat; movements that had never occurred before. The only way that I controlled my terror was by singing the Psalms during this 13-mile-trip. I refused to have anything to do with this practice. It was my understanding that I should "resist the Devil," not draw close to him.

I now believe this was the closest to the spiritual world of evil that I had ever come. I now believe that the spirit of Satan had entered into Yisrayl Hawkins when he opened himself up to this demonic influence.

The Golden Age

The years 1987 through 1990 marked the golden age for The House of Yahweh for several reasons. This is when Yisrayl Hawkins began to travel extensively and speak at different locations. His first engagement, in February, 1987, was in Manitowoc, Wisconsin, accompanied by Elder Walter Jandrisevits and our daughter, DeeDee. This meeting was very successful. When *The Book of Yahweh* was finished in 1987, I began to go with him. In January, 1988, we visited Phoenix, Arizona, and in May of 1988 we were in Missouri. We visited Hawaii in February of 1989; in August, 1989, we were on the island of Trinidad in the West Indies. Two weeks later we were in Toronto, Ontario, Canada. In December, 1989, we visited in Tennessee. There were also several informal visits to Louisiana. Each of these visits brought in new members and the sanctuary building in Abilene began to be filled to maximum capacity. Then abruptly, these visits stopped.

The House of Yahweh was actually a wonderful place to be during this time. This was a "new movement," unlike any others that I knew about. It was a place where one could "prove all things and hold fast to the right way." Since we were a house, we were also Yahweh's Family and our instructions were to treat each other with honor and respect, as sisters and brothers, mothers and fathers, with all purity. Every time that a new member came in, he or she was welcomed as a new brother or sister. The feasts were celebrated like great family reunions. There were marriages and new babies, parties, events, wonderful memories. Very rarely was there a funeral. The family was growing and I was part of it. There was a sense of belonging, and of commitment to a high and great purpose. One felt accepted and validated.

This was the era in which there were white wall tents covering the area behind the Sanctuary in Abilene as the feasts were in progress. Trailer hookups were also installed for those who had travel trailers. A large, bright and cheerful, red and yellow tent covered the parking lot. Folding chairs were set up, as well as the sound system. A Hearing Interpreter was employed for our hearing impaired members. The tent was filled to maximum capacity. Yisrayl Hawkins visited with everyone on the feast grounds. The sermons presented by the Elders were inspired and wonderful.

Spokesmen classes were formed for the men and women, because it was discovered during this time that women were speakers in the era of the Apostles,[28] and one of the women actually was an Apostle.[29] [11]

Yisrayl preached a sermon entitled, "Marriage Yahweh's Way," in 1989, which promoted monogamy in marriage and the elevation of women from that of a household slave to a partner at a man's side; a "helper suitable." There would be wonderful opportunities for both men and women in The House of Yahweh.

Yisrayl preached that The House of Yahweh would be a part of Rebuilding the Temple in Jerusalem. Due to extensive research of the Temple's dimensions when The Book of Yahweh was being typeset, it was proposed that the Temple could be built without infringing on the property upon which the Moslem Mosque was set. Yisrayl made trips to Israel on March 18, 1988, and on May 26, 1989, with this message; to whom he spoke I do not remember.

The House of Yahweh Choir was organized and our songbook was in the final stages of development. *The Book Of The Songs Of Praise To Yahweh, A House of Yahweh Publication®TM,* would be copyrighted in 1990. Our printing press was running five days a week publishing the books, booklets, bibles, and songbooks which were being sent throughout the United States, Canada, Mexico, the Caribbean, and Europe. Everyone had a purpose. We were focused on helping proclaim the message of The Kingdom of Yahweh to all the world. We all could barely wait for the Messiah to return.

DeeDee's Wedding

The Feast of Pentecost was scheduled for Sabbath, June 10, 1989, so the date chosen for DeeDee's wedding was set for Sunday, June 11, 1989. The months leading up to her marriage were filled with planning for this event, as well as for the Feast of Pentecost. Since the large red and

---

28   Acts 21:9, Phillip had four virgin daughters who prophesied.
29   Romans 16:7, Junia, wife of Andronicus; both were Apostles.

yellow tent would already be set up for the feast, this would be the area for the reception after the ceremony.

All of the Elders were involved, as were their wives. All of the Deacons and Deaconesses, and all the people helped in one way or another. This was a lavish affair. I also invited my dad to the ceremony. He came and enjoyed himself. DeeDee was beautiful in her long white dress. Her bridesmaids were dressed in blue satin. Her husband was dressed in a black suit with a satin blue tie, wearing a white shirt, tallit and kippah. The groomsmen were dressed in black suits and ties, with white shirts, tallits, and kippahs. The ceremony was performed by Yisrayl Hawkins, while the bride and groom stood under the canopy. The groom stomped the wineglass into a zillion slivers. Afterward, everyone retired to the tent for the reception and blessing. DeeDee and her new husband went on a carriage ride, compliments of one of the members. A dance followed later in the evening. I remember that Daddy danced with DeeDee, as also did Yisrayl Hawkins. I felt content and blessed.

This was not the first wedding in The House of Yahweh, but it was the first wedding that I had planned for one of my children. Dennis was married to his beautiful wife before this event, but their wedding was performed in the bride's mother's home. Yisrayl and I were invited, but he did not attend. However, I went to see my son and his new wife. I rejoiced with my son on his wedding day, even though he still remained outside The House of Yahweh at the time. I prayed that he would return someday.

I was not able to attend my son David's wedding to his beautiful wife. I was excommunicated from The House of Yahweh when the ceremony was performed in the sanctuary in 1994. I have beautiful pictures of this event, but I missed not being there to celebrate with him. I prayed that one day I would have all of my children with me.

The Forty-Four

It was in January, 1988, that events came about to obtain land in Eula, Texas, which would eventually come to be known as "The Forty-Four" or "The Protected Place." The large sanctuary would eventually be constructed upon this property, and this is how we obtained this land.

A young couple in the congregation had set up a dummy sale of their inherited, homesteaded land to another couple. At this time it was impossible to borrow capital against a homestead in Texas. The proceeds of this sale went toward purchasing a computer business in Abilene, with the other couple managing the business. Well, their business failed, and the bank which loaned money to the business began the process of repossessing their land, which was the collateral.

They went to see Yisrayl for help. Yisrayl agreed to pay off their debt. On August 3, 1988, the couple signed a Contract of Sale with Yisrayl and Kay Hawkins so they could buy back their property. The note began with a $2,000.00 down payment. The young couple made payments of $400.00 per month beginning June 1, 1988. They made these payments through October 30, 1989, and then they decided that they could not continue. On December 20, 1989, their contract was declared null and void and this land reverted to the personal property of Yisrayl and Kay Hawkins.

When "The Forty-Four," located on Oak Forest Road, returned to our possession, Yisrayl decided to move the organization of The House of Yahweh onto this property. There were no zoning laws or building restrictions to bother with in the country; he could build where and how he pleased.

Members were already living in the houses and mobile homes that we had built or set up on our property on Highway 603. This Eula property on the open highway, upon which the Pressroom and Yliyah School was also situated, was becoming known as "Yahweh Village."

It was around the beginning of January, 1990, that the campaign began in earnest to move the sanctuary from Abilene to Eula. The scripture from Micah 4:10, *The Book of Yahweh, Second Printing*, was used to prophesy about the venture,

> …For now you will go forth out of the "city," and you will live in the "field," and you will go to "Babylon." There you will be delivered; there Yahweh will redeem you from the hand of your enemies.

During the sermons it was explained that the "city" we would leave was Abilene, Texas. We would live for a while in the "field," otherwise revealed to be the properties in the Eula area. It was preached from the pulpit that there was a city in New York State named Babylon. The rationale was that The House of Yahweh organization would leave Abilene, move to Eula, and would eventually go to Babylon, New York. From there, the people of The House of Yahweh would be delivered to the place of safety in Jerusalem.

The construction of the new sanctuary for The House of Yahweh was started in the spring of 1990. Elder David Mrotek and Elder Don Stenz, from Wisconsin, temporarily moved into their own mobile homes which were already set up on The Forty Four, and supervised its completion.

The work crews were all members of The House of Yahweh and performed all aspects of its construction: plumbing, electrical, concrete, ironwork, carpentry, and finishing. Kitchen crews were also organized to ensure that the workers were fed. The construction went smoothly, with no down time until it was completed.

Every word in the scriptures has a meaning. The word, "Babylon," according to *Strong's Exhaustive Concordance,* means "Confusion."

This is exactly what happened. Long before Yisrayl Hawkins began the process of leaving Abilene and moving The House of Yahweh sanctuary to The Forty-Four, Yisrayl Hawkins began to be led into a progressive state of absolute spiritual confusion.

An organization is only as sound as its leadership. Since Yisrayl Hawkins was the leader, the projects that he personally managed after this began to show the "fruit" of what his mind had already become.

Unknown to all of us, the winds of change were in the air. This "mixture of righteousness and evil" started to become evident in 1989, when the growth of The House of Yahweh was at its most profound. Gossip and rumors rippled throughout the congregation about Yisrayl and other women. When I confronted him about these accusations, Yisrayl would look me right in the eye and say, "I will never sin." He never once said, "I did not do it."

I wanted to believe my husband; remember his "vow" to me? So, I believed him and defended him against all who came against him.

Yisrayl also refused to relinquish any of his power or delegate any of his authority or responsibility as growth continued. There were intelligent leaders in the congregation who could have successfully executed these responsibilities—Elders who were wise and greatly respected.

Yisrayl refused to make decisions which would have expanded the leadership of the organization; which would have encompassed more dynamic growth; which would have established a foundation of fiscal responsibility and positive public relations.

Instead, true to form, Yisrayl Hawkins continued to follow his same old pattern of absolute power and control. Just as customary, he lost interest in watching over the important little details, which would eventually cause The House of Yahweh to become known as the largest doomsday cult in America, not the greatest religion in the world.

CHAPTER THIRTEEN

1990
A Curse Causeless Does Not Come

The woman who would become Yisrayl's "new friend," my other "her," was ordained as a Deaconess on April 17, 1990, the last Holy Day of the Feast of Unleavened Bread, which was still being held in Abilene.

I don't know the date or time that "she" found out that Yisrayl Hawkins was a prejudiced bigot. When she did find out, as I later learned, since she was also black, that she marched right into his office and straightened him out. Blacks would not be segregated into the Congo of the New World, and she would certainly see to it.

There was an amazing change in Yisrayl's attitude toward blacks beginning about this time. Yisrayl began promoting interracial marriages, and officiated during several of the ceremonies. I approved of this desegregation. I did not approve of the gossip and rumors that still rippled throughout the congregation about Yisrayl and other women. "Don't believe the gossip," he would say to me, and I wanted to believe they were lies. Where there is smoke, there is fire, but I just did not want to see it.

Also about this same time, spring of 1990, Yisrayl told me that he was needed at all times, so now he was moving out of our home to be closer to "the work." I thought it was because construction on the new sanctuary was still in progress and that he would come home afterward.

He had set up a small mobile home on the Abilene property with an office attached to the front. He also arranged to move another mobile home onto The Forty Four where he also stayed. I was to do the work of getting The Prophetic Word ready for printing, for making the taped sermon copies and getting them ready to be sent out, for maintaining the mailing list, for keeping the financial books for The House of Yahweh, for rebutting Jacob O. Meyer's opposition which was still going on at this time, and for anything else that needed to be done. Yisrayl would come home twice a week, on Wednesday night to go out to dinner and on Friday evening when I prepared dinner for him and invited our children and guests, and to attend services on the Sabbath.

I was alone with my work and my two youngest children, Margo and Justin. Thankfully, my youngest son, Justin, was allowed to remain with me in my home. He was not forced to leave as were my two older sons, Dennis and David.

At the same time whisperings and gossip about Yisrayl and other women were going around in the congregation, rumors and gossip about some of the members of The House of Yahweh were also circulating in the local community. Yisrayl Hawkins had taken on this responsibility, but he had become bored with the responsibility of dealing with these mentally handicapped people. They lived in two dilapidated mobile homes facing Eula Highway 603, along with several large dogs which were not house trained.

It would have been best if these people had resided at the back of the property. But no, they set right on the highway where everyone who drove by could see them.

Yisrayl always said there is "no such thing as bad publicity." I could not help but think when he said this, "Have you forgotten your police days?" The first media blitz focused on the badly dilapidated mobile home occupied by three mentally handicapped men and their imprisoned dogs. The lifestyle of these men and animals was viewed as a filthy stinking mess. By association, so was The House of Yahweh. This image and perception would continue to grow as time went on.

Public scrutiny began to narrowly focus on Yisrayl Hawkins when he tried to become the "public relations man" for The House of Yahweh. On Saturday, May 5, 1990, an extensive article was written on the first page of Section E, the Religion Section of *The Abilene Reporter News,* by Roy A. Jones II, Religion Editor. This article is entitled, *House of Yahweh, Abilene is "world headquarters" for misunderstood religious group,* and begins,

> Of all the religious sects worshipping in Abilene, the most misunderstood has to be the House of Yahweh.
>
> Its followers are aware of the many rumors, but have done little to dispel them. Instead, they say they prefer to concentrate on trying to follow all the laws of Yahweh, the Creator to whom most other religions refer as God.
>
> Few outsiders know what really goes on inside the tall, privacy fence that surrounds "The Land of Yahweh" at 1025 T&P Lane in southeast Abilene.
>
> But lots of people obviously have conjured up images ranging from Satan worship and animal sacrifices to an opportunist, religion-for-profit scam that brainwashes converts and breaks up families.
>
> Nothing could be further from the truth, says Elder Yisrayl Hawkins, the House of Yahweh's pastor and overseer.

The most damaging was a separate article beginning on Page 2-E, also dated May 5, 1990, and also written by Roy A. Jones II, entitled, *Rumors don't worry House of Yahweh leader.*

When Yisrayl stated to Roy Jones, "Rumors don't worry The House of Yahweh," this started the local citizens to worry even more. They became extremely suspicious of a man who didn't care about the image of the religious organization that he was trying to promote.

Yisrayl, with his current mindset, considered these articles to be "positive publicity." However, they insinuated that everyone but members of The House of Yahweh were pagans who were headed straight to hell for going to church on Sunday. Really positive, isn't it?

Well, Yisrayl immediately produced advertising spots on KTAB television in which he was the "star." These spots began on May 28 and ended on June 8, 1990. Rather than being perceived by the viewing public as a sincere religious leader, these productions made Yisrayl Hawkins appear to be an arrogant, conceited con-artist, luring the suckers in for the scam.

It was not three weeks later, June 22, 1990, that Bob Roebuck, a reporter for KTAB television, requested an interview with Yisrayl. Roebuck had just come from a residence near Eula where he heard the complaint of a local citizen against his next door neighbor. The interview is stated to have gone like this:

Yisrayl—"What can I do for you?"
Roebuck—"Do you own some land north of Eula?"
Yisrayl—"Yes we do."
Roebuck—"Is it called Yahweh Village?"
Yisrayl—"Not to my knowledge. Why, is something wrong?"
Roebuck—"Some of the neighbors say the people who live there are dirty, nasty people."
Yisrayl—"Who are you referring to?"
Roebuck—"Those on the south end."
Yisrayl—"If you are referring to the widow woman with three sons, I agree they need help, and we have made arrangements to help them clean up. We have bought them a new mobile home and are looking for another."
Roebuck—'Yes, they're the ones."
Yisrayl—"We have also formed a committee to help this family stay clean after we get them moved in. But you are surely not going to insinuate that retarded people are typical of all House of Yahweh people, are you?"
Roebuck—"No, we are not going to do that, but we did notice that some of the mobile homes were old trailers and some of the lawns were not mowed."
Yisrayl—"Did you look across the street? That twelve acres has about ten junked cars on it, trash all over the place, and hasn't been mowed all year. Are they (the neighbor who complained about the mess) complaining about that house? It's owned by a member of the Church of Christ. Will you call that a Church of Christ Village? If you call the land to the east "Yahweh Village" because some members of the House of Yahweh live there and you do not call the land to the west "Church of Christ Village," then that's religious persecution. The one doing the complaining is not totally clean himself, and has not previously kept his lawn mowed, nor his trash picked up. He even raised hogs in his back yard, which stank up the whole neighborhood. He burns trash

on a regular basis and runs waste water in his back yard. There is trash galore behind his old pallet fence. For him to complain about anyone would be like the pot calling the kettle black. It is our understanding that he goes to the Baptist Church in Eula."

Roebuck—"They seem to be down on the House of Yahweh. What do you think is causing this?"

Yisrayl—"It is my opinion that they just don't understand the teachings of The House of Yahweh."

When the interview was aired on KTAB, the news caster started with "Callahan County Citizens complain about cleanliness of House of Yahweh Village." The complaining neighbor stated on camera, "They live with dogs and the place stinks." Yisrayl's statement followed, "They just don't understand the teachings of the House of Yahweh."

This sounded just like The House of Yahweh, led by Yisrayl Hawkins, condoned living with dogs in a stinking mess, and that the neighbor's complaint constituted "religious persecution."

Another article was published in *The Abilene Reporter News,* this time reporting on the massive cleanup prompted by the newscast. Well, now that the public was involved this lit a fire under Yisrayl Hawkins which prompted the cleanup. It is regretful that the place was not kept clean for very long.

A letter of rebuttal against this newscast was compiled by Yisrayl and his office staff and sent to the citizens of Abilene. In this letter, Yisrayl stated,

> It was never the intent of the House of Yahweh to go to the public with our beliefs. We have always followed the example of the apostle Paul who taught all who came to him. We have never tried to force our beliefs on others and it is not our intent to do so at this time. However, we must defend ourselves by letting the public know we are not what the news media painted us to be in their "Christian" attack against us.

Yisrayl's psychotic rant against their "Christian attack against us" only served to antagonize the public even further. I ask you now, if "It was never the intent of the House of Yahweh to go to the public with our beliefs..." why did Yisrayl Hawkins relate almost every belief and doctrine of the organization, which were clearly written in the May 5, 1990, articles in *The Abilene Reporter News?* Why did he portray himself as a rock star during the KTAB advertising spots?

Remember, true to form, nothing is ever Yisrayl's fault. Rather than admit that he had made a huge media blunder, and put himself forward as the leader of the organization to take the heat, Yisrayl Hawkins hid himself behind every man, woman and child in the congregation. He stood in the pulpit, and screamed, "We are being persecuted!!"

Yisrayl placed them out in front to accept the responsibility and guilt for the decisions, and comments, that he had personally made. Many of the members, deeply embarrassed and personally offended, wrote letters defending The House of Yahweh because of this manipulation.

At almost the same time, Yisrayl put his foot in his mouth again and caused another session of "no such thing as bad publicity" for the congregation. Remember, Yisrayl liked Eula because there were no zoning laws or building restrictions to worry about. He did not factor-in eventually being sued by The State of Texas for running a non-compliant water system facility.

On July 24, 1990, there was an "official inspection" of Yahweh Village Sewer Systems, over which Charles Keith, Registered Sanitarian with the State of Texas, and Braxton Bryant, Sanitarian in Training, presided. They were accompanied by Elder J.E. Martin. The sewer systems were deemed to be "properly functioning" and "legal" after the inspection.

As soon as the tour was completed, Keith asked, "What about the water out here?"

Martin: "There is (sic) 4 or 5 wells individually owned by the residents who share the wells on the tracts."

Keith: "This is a public water system."

Elder J.E. Martin allowed them to take water samples from two wells, which were found to contain no harmful compounds. This did not prevent Keith from designating the entire water system on Highway 603 as Hawkins Subdivision Water System Facility. The article, "Yahweh septic tanks flush with law as far as inspection can tell," written by Ramona Ney, ran in *The Abilene Reporter News,* Saturday, July 28, 1990.

Now it was "Yahweh" septic tanks, not "Hawkins" septic tanks. Excerpts from this article state,

> At a June 25 meeting, some area residents asked that the Callahan County Commissioners take action on the growing number of House of Yahweh settlements. Some residents living near the group said they feared improperly installed septic tanks might contaminate area water wells...
>
> House of Yahweh Pastor Yisrayl Hawkins, who owns some of the land in question, said that his congregation was being persecuted by people who were ignorant about the group's beliefs. The county officials took no action because they said they had no control over development in rural areas...
>
> Because Hawkins appears to be supplying water to at least 25 people at the FM 603 site, Hawkins will be classified by the health department as a public water system, Keith said.
>
> This classification will require Hawkins to install a chlorination system that will pump small amounts of bleach water into the site's five water wells, and Hawkins must submit bacteriological samples from the wells monthly to the health department, Keith said.

Rather than being open and above-board, and actually communicating with Charles Keith and the Texas Department of Health, Hawkins isolated himself and again began to scream "persecution" from the pulpit. It was again the people's fault, never his own.

It would have been far better if Hawkins had just contacted Keith to see how fast this situation could be resolved. Instead, Yisrayl turned to Attorney H. Bryce Parker III in July to initiate communication with Keith and the State of Texas.

On July 19, 1991, Bill Hawkins, not Yisrayl Hawkins, was served with Citation 91-9606, in which he was being sued by The State of Texas Department of Health for operating a non-compliant public water system, Hawkins Subdivision Public Water Supply in Eula, Texas, for approximately 48 persons.

I was involved with the appeals, documentation, etc. from the time we were sued until the time this was resolved. Contracts of Sale were filed with the County Clerk in Baird, Texas, proving that this land had been sold.

There was also another round of listening to Yisrayl preach, "they're picking on us," which was meant to involve the members of the congregation on the front lines of resistance. Attorney Gary Brown represented Yisrayl Hawkins in 1991. The rumors about illegal drugs and guns on The House of Yahweh property floated around the community without ceasing.

Yisrayl's next blunder quickly revolved around a family from New Mexico. They initially came to the Feast of Pentecost in 1989, when I met their oldest children first. They were trying to hurt some of our younger children who were playing on the merry-go-round. When I saw the danger, I went over and told two young men, who were in their mid-teens, to stop spinning the wheel so fast. They ignored me, laughed, and finally ran away. My first impression of them was that they were anti-social misfits.

They did not come to the Feast of Tabernacles because the family could not get excused absences from school for their children. It would be later that I learned that Yisrayl decided that he wanted The House of Yahweh to become the Plaintiff in a legal suit against their school district, citing "religious persecution." He hired a New Mexico attorney to begin the lawsuit.

Yisrayl only informed me at the time that this family was moving to Abilene. I informed him not allow them to move close to the sanctuary because they would tear it up.

Later, I found a letter addressed to me in my position as Principle, House of Yahweh School, dated January 29, 1990. Yisrayl never gave this letter to me. This letter was from the opposing attorney for the New Mexico school district in question. The letter requested information about Yliyah School.

Instead of Yisrayl giving this letter to me, Yisrayl assigned this to his trusted associate, Elder J. E. Martin. He knew that I would have responded truthfully to the opposing attorney's requests about information concerning Yliyah School. I would have informed the opposing attorney that we were not accredited with the State of Texas, but our curriculum was excellent.

Some of the older children in this family were performing far below grade level and were in special education classes, so Yisrayl Hawkins didn't want to take on this much responsibility.

Instead, he instructed Elder Martin to contact the administrator of the Clyde School District, and ask him to respond to the opposing attorney's request for information. These children subsequently were enrolled in the Clyde School District, not in the Yliyah School.

In March, 1990, Yisrayl also decided to move this family right into the middle of the city of Clyde, Texas. The family had a two year lease.

The children didn't go to school regularly, and no one in the family was gainfully employed. The older boys would ride around on bicycles during school hours, get into mischief, and when caught or pursued would shout to the top of their lungs, "Praise Yahweh!!"

Their actions greatly angered me, so I know that the citizens of Clyde were equally outraged.

All of the honest, hard working, responsible people in the congregation of The House of Yahweh were being humiliated by their unrestrained antics. Rather than help these people move into an isolated corner at the back of a mesquite tree pasture, which would have been a better fit for their lifestyle, Yisrayl defended them.

What was he thinking? Was this done in spite or was this another manifestation of his reprobate mind? Yisrayl Hawkins made the conscious decision to defend them— and not to defend the honest, hard-working members of the congregation who were being embarrassed by them.

Because of this, the citizens of the local community associated this family and their irresponsible behavior with The House of Yahweh, including that of "illegal drugs."

Of course, it was not Yisrayl's fault that he had made a really bad decision about taking this family under his wings. It had to be the really bad publicity about a sect leader in Florida who had given himself the name, Yahweh ben Yahweh.

The shadow of that publicity, Yisrayl had convinced himself, was darkening the image of our organization. A letter of rebuttal was composed and was published in the January 10, 1991, issue of *The Clyde Journal*.

We had hoped that this would have dispelled any fears anyone might have had about The House of Yahweh, but the damage was already done. Every effort to allay the citizens' fears was met with suspicion and distrust. The family from New Mexico left town in the spring of 1991.

Just about the time this crisis was beginning, another crisis loomed on the horizon, and again I was given another assignment. I was to help Yisrayl Hawkins to establish a "Security Guard Service" for The House of Yahweh. This is what I was told at the beginning. I would eventually learn that Yisrayl Hawkins wanted an "armed" security guard service.

Yisrayl had already formed a security guard unit for The House of Yahweh around 1988. These guards were called the Shamarim, the Watchmen. Their duties were innocent enough: night watchmen during the feasts, guards at the entrance gate, personal guards for Yisrayl Hawkins. This was innocent enough, that is, until Yisrayl decided he wanted the guards to be "armed," and applied for their licenses to carry firearms.

Bill W. Skinner, in his capacity as Sheriff of Callahan County, sent a letter of protest for this venture to the Executive Director, Texas Board of Private Investigators, in Austin, Texas. This letter, dated October 4, 1990, states,

> I do protest the carrying of weapons at church or on church properties. I really don't feel there is a need for armed guards in these areas.

It was on October 9, 1990, that Ronald L. Young, in his capacity as Chief of Police with the Clyde Police Department, sent a letter of objection to the Texas Board of Private Investigators and Private Security Agencies, stating,

> There is a group of House of Yahweh people residing inside the corporate city limits of Clyde, Texas. They have claimed this residence as a place of worship, a church, and I strongly protest the presence of these persons being armed guards in Clyde. These people represent themselves as being a religion and steadfast in the observance of The Lords Word but our department has had several contacts with this group in our official capacity and several arrests have been made.

Yisrayl was determined that the Shamarim would become "armed guards," and pursued this through the legal system. On August 21, 1991, depositions were taken from Clyde Police Chief Ronald L. Young and County Sheriff Bill Skinner by Yisrayl's attorney, who then was Gary Brown:

Young: "My objection was that it is not common practice to have armed security guards for any particular church. We haven't issued one for or hadn't had a request for Church of Christ, Baptist, Methodist, Lion's Club, Kiwanis, whatever. And I didn't think it was necessary and that is why I objected."

Brown: "Okay. And that is the only reason you objected?"

Young: "That's correct. And if I recall correctly, it was armed security, am I correct?"

Brown: "…Yes, these individuals are asking the Agency to issue them a security office commission to be able to carry a firearm."

Brown: "Okay. Have you talked to anybody from The House of Yahweh that told you what kind of security company or whatever they are going to be doing under their letter of authority?"

Skinner: "I talked to Bill Hawkins, he called me about it when I protested."

Brown: "Okay. And?"

Skinner: "He told me that he needed armed guards because they had irrational people coming to these places and people got out of control. And I just made the statement to Bill, You know, I've been to a lot of revivals and stuff like that and I haven't seen the need of armed guards in a place of worship, and I might knock it down to that."

Brown: "Okay. So, your biggest objection is…if they get their security office commissions, carrying their weapon from their home to whatever that place is?"

Skinner: "Well, just wearing their weapons out, I just don't think in a situation like this that any organization like that needs armed guards. I say, "security," yes, but not "armed security guards.""

These peace officers of Callahan County were absolutely correct in their opposition to "armed security guards" in a religious organization, and especially The House of Yahweh.

Why would a religious leader think for one moment that he needed "armed guards?" Was this another manipulation to make Yisrayl feel powerful? The citizens of Callahan County began to become even more suspicious and fearful of Yisrayl Hawkins' true motives.

The Feast of Tabernacles and Last Great Day were scheduled for October 5 through 12, 1990. After the feast was over and we were returning to our regular work schedule, Yisrayl came to me and said that his little personal secretary had stolen some money from The House of Yahweh and that he couldn't use her in the office any longer.

This was very strange, since Yisrayl knew that she had a weakness in this area. About five years earlier Yisrayl had brought a series of sermons, entitled *Lying and Betrayal in The House of Yahweh,* which stressed the importance of keeping confidences relating to the whereabouts of any member, her in particular at the time. She had been arrested for theft by fraud and was sent to prison for several months. We kept her two children in our home during the time she was incarcerated. When she was released from prison, she became the secretary in the front office in Abilene.

How did this happen? She was so faithful for so long. She was relieved of her duties about the end of November, 1990.

December of 1990 is also when Yisrayl's "new friend" moved to Abilene. The first thing I can remember about this was when a small utility trailer was pulled onto my home property in Eula. I asked Yisrayl who this belonged to. He named "her," and also stated that she was now his new front office secretary.

I smelled a rat. The fetid stench of Yisrayl Hawkins and his immoral manipulations to get her to Abilene became apparent to me. "No," Yisrayl said, "It's not what you think. She came to do the work of Yahweh."

At the same time, December of 1990, while I was grateful to Yahweh that our name, The House of Yahweh, had been saved from the clutches of Jacob O. Meyer and his Assemblies of Yahweh, was my pain and humiliation about Yisrayl Hawkins and his new secretary, my new "her."

CHAPTER FOURTEEN

1991
Jacob's Death,
The New Sanctuary is Dedicated

The year, 1991, started with Yisrayl purchasing a really nice mobile home for "her" to live in, and had it placed on the Abilene sanctuary property directly across from him. I was not consulted about this purchase, or about any other purchases that Yisrayl Hawkins would be making from this time forward. Thereafter, I later learned, money was spent to construct a covered veranda on the front of her trailer, where she and Yisrayl could barbeque in the evenings. I was never invited to her home for dinner or I would have seen the evidence of his presence.

The gossip now started about her and Yisrayl. She was still a married woman at the time. She would eventually sue her husband for divorce, and would affirm that she was not gainfully employed. Therefore, she was not able to pay any child support for her two sons, whom she abandoned to the care of their father.

Of course, when I confronted Yisrayl about the gossip, it was the same glib comments, "I will never sin." "Don't believe the gossip."

Did I start to see the truth? Subconsciously I did; shortly after "her" arrival I had a very vivid dream that Yisrayl had left me. Consciously, I was in a state of complete denial. I was unable to accept the fact that I was being victimized, used, and deceived. I would continue to defend him because I did not want to face the reality of being conned and manipulated. I refused to acknowledge his abuse as a means of self-protection.[30]

I was completely unable to get through to him that what he was doing was wrong. He had no concept of the consequences of his actions. He also thought of himself as fully entitled, and he was going to do whatever he wanted.[31] It did not help the situation that he calmed his nerves and clouded his mind with shots of peach brandy on every appropriate occasion.

Around the beginning of February, Jacob's oldest son called Yisrayl and told him that Jacob was dying of pancreatic cancer, and was now in an Odessa hospital awaiting the inevitable.

I later learned that both Jacob and Isabel objected to him calling, but since Yisrayl was "family" he decided to call him anyway. Jacob did not summon Yisrayl, and it was not his desire to see Yisrayl before he died—as Yisrayl had led me and everyone else to believe. Jacob also physically removed Yisrayl's hand from his head during a prayer for his healing.

Yisrayl was panic-stricken. It was not that Jacob was on his deathbed, it was the fact that Yisrayl's sermons about "The Two Witnesses" would be proven to be false. I had never seen Yisrayl Hawkins so restless before. He paced; he drank peach brandy in excess.

He drove to Odessa on three occasions to see Jacob—the first time taking "her" and another woman with him.

Isabel later told me that the second time Yisrayl came to visit Jacob, he said that he would fast and pray for Jacob's recovery. After Yisrayl left the room, Jacob's two youngest sons and others went out to stand on the hospital balcony. A few moments later, one of their sons said, "Look down here." Yisrayl had parked his car on their side of the hospital, and when they looked down, they saw Yisrayl walking to his car while carrying a large drink in a cup and eating popcorn from a bag. Jacob's second son said, "If that's fasting, we're going to get some popcorn and a drink on Yom Kippur." Isabel said they all laughed about Yisrayl's notion of "fasting and praying."

March 22, 1991, was the day of Jacob's death. The announcement

---

30   *Take Back Your Life*, Janja Lalich and Madeleine Tobias, "Callousness and Lack of Empathy," pages 64-65.

31   *Take Back Your Life*, "Grandiose Sense of Self," page 62.

was published in the March, 1991, issue of *The Prophetic Watchman,* beginning on page 22,

> The Prophetic Watchman has been the publication work of the House of Yahweh since its beginning in Nazareth, Israel in 1973 and its move to Odessa, Texas in 1975. The reason that it has not been getting out as regularly as normal in recent months is because of a severe tragedy that Yahweh's work has been undergoing. In November of 1990, the Overseer of the House of Yahweh and Editor of The Prophetic Watchman, Jacob Hawkins, began to suffer a serious sickness which had him in and out of the hospital. As this announcement is being written, the date is March 24, 1991. It is with utmost grief that we must now inform our readers that on March 22, a Friday, and by the Hebrew calendar Nissan 7, 5751, Jacob passed away. His burial was held that afternoon, just before the Sabbath.

Yisrayl stated that he went to the funeral, his third and final trip to see Jacob. Yisrayl testified to Jacob's family that he had lain on Jacob's body in the funeral home in order to resurrect him, but Jacob's second son said that no one witnessed this event. Yisrayl's niece stated that he caused some sort of scene at the graveside service, and left before it was over.

I did not go because I was not invited. The Passover and Feast of Unleavened Bread was from March 30 through April 6, 1991, only a few days after Jacob's death. This was being held in Abilene, since the sanctuary in Eula was still under construction.

Yisrayl was sweating bullets. He knew he was going to have to announce Jacob's death to the Abilene congregation. This would not have been difficult except that he also knew that his preaching about "The Two Witnesses" would soon be revealed as "false prophecy" coming from a "false prophet."

This was a pivotal moment in The House of Yahweh. We had two choices before us, humility or pride. We could have admitted that we were wrong about the prophecy of The Two Witnesses, apologized to Yahweh and to His people, and continued to preach His word. The spiritual foundation of the organization was in place. Even Jacob O. Meyer would not be able to stop the publishing of The House of

Yahweh. Instead, we took the path of "pride." The "fruits" thereafter speak for themselves.

The Feast of Unleavened Bread began normally, or so it seemed outwardly. The people were enjoying the fellowship and the sermons; no drama yet. Yisrayl had a secret meeting with the Elders and informed them of Jacob's death. They were to be prepared for the outburst which would surely come. Yisrayl's sermons were slowly building for the bad announcement. When Yisrayl finally dropped the bomb that Jacob had died, you could hear a pin drop. We waited for the explosion.

Several people believed the scriptures—and left The House of Yahweh, Abilene—which say in Deuteronomy 18:20-22, *The Book of Yahweh, Second Printing,* page 162,

> 20. But a prophet who presumes to speak a word in My Name, which I have not commanded him to say, or who speaks in the name of any god, that prophet must be put to death.
> 21. And you may say to yourself; How can we know when a message has not been spoken by Yahweh?
> 22. If what a prophet proclaims in the Name of Yahweh, does not come to pass, or does not come true: that is a message Yahweh has not spoken. That prophet has spoken presumptuously. Do not follow him at all.

Yisrayl Hawkins knows these scriptures. He proceeded afterward to chuckle and laugh from the pulpit, proclaim that he was "just a mere man," and now he had come to new and better understanding of the scriptures. Thereafter, *The Two Witnesses* booklet was rewritten, with the help of many others, me included. The "new light" was the scripture in Isaiah (Isayah) 43:28, rewritten in 1991:

> Therefore, I will dissolve the Levitical Priesthood; and will give Yaaqob to the curse and Yisrayl to reproaches.

Of course, the curse given to Yaaqob was death, and the "one remaining witness," Yisrayl, was given to "reproaches". These "reproaches" are not slurs spoken against the man. These were presented as words of "mocking the law of Yahweh." Yisrayl accepted this with the greatest conceit. Now, when outsiders "persecuted" Yisrayl, they were actually mocking Yahweh. This was great! It was not his fault he was being reproached and persecuted. It was their fault because they hated Yahweh's Laws!

Another thing grieved me about Jacob's death. We had been notified that Jacob O. Meyer had dropped his Trademark Opposition against the House of Yahweh on December 20, 1990, but it was not until April 16, 1991, that we received the Certificate of Registration for our Trademark, HOUSE OF YAHWEH. Jacob Hawkins did not live to see this.

The first service in the new sanctuary on The Forty Four, which came to be known as The Protected Place, was on the Sabbath Day, May 18, 1991. I remember this day very well. Yisrayl had his personal office in the building with a waiting room in front of it. When I came back to his office I saw "her" with him, in his office and not sitting in the reception area where her place was. I threw a fit and demanded that she get her ass out of there, that this was terrible, that this is why the people were gossiping, and this needed to stop, now.

Yisrayl had a glazed, faraway look on his face as he calmly told me that there was nothing wrong, that he needed a personal secretary, and it was me who told him that she did a great job working in the store during a previous feast. Now it was my fault that she was here.

I was unable to say anything that penetrated Yisrayl's mind to make him understand. The fact that he was sipping peach brandy from his coffee cup may have contributed to his lack of reality. It was as though he were a robot, without any feelings at all. I was not wrong about this.

The Yliyah School held their graduation ceremony in the new sanctuary on May 19, 1991. There were six Kindergarten and two High School graduates.

May 20, 1991, at 1:00 in the afternoon, the first wedding was performed in the new sanctuary.

On May 20, 1991, at sunset, began the first feast which was celebrated on The Protected Place—the Feast of Pentecost which continued through May 21, 1991, at sunset. My daughter, Margo, was betrothed in the afternoon on this date.

I was taking on the same spirit of hatred and hostility that Yisrayl carried on a pedestal. A letter was sent to Yisrayl from one of the members, dated July 14, 1991. Yisrayl came to me, deceptively inferring that he was being accused of dishonesty, and that she was requesting a Financial Report because of it. Since I kept the books at the time, it was me who was being accused. I sent her a very hateful letter on June 17, along with the Financial Report. She sent such a kind and humble letter to me. Her words speak to me from the past, and I would like to share a few of them with you,

> Shalom Kay,
> Thank you for the financial report…
>
> I don't know what smoke screen you are talking about as (her husband) know (sic) where I stand and there are some people in the House of Yahweh knows (sic) that I don't really believe that Yisrayl is one of the two witnesses and I am almost sure that you, two (sic) are aware of that…I must be careful about accepting man's interpretating (sic) of Scriptures. I must study things thoroughly before I either swallow or spit the teaching out. No one should expect me to accept anything without question, as I am not that kind of person who believe (sic) anything that any person said as a fact.
>
> I don't know why you call my asking for the report an accusation. I think making an accusation without any solid proof is an insanity (sic) thing to do. There is one thing I have learned is that reading between lines and jumping to conclusions doesn't really make things better but only makes things more worse.
>
> If running the office dealing with buying supplies is getting too much for you or you are heading for a burnout…then I suggest that you delegate the responsibility to someone who would consider it a great service to Yahweh, without pay.

She set me down hard. I sincerely pray that she accepts my sincere apology should she read this. It would only be a very short time later that "she," Yisrayl's "new friend" and secretary, would take over the financial books for The House of Yahweh.

The money coming in was delegated to her and Yisrayl. Only they would really know how much money was coming in, or how much was being spent thereafter.

When Yisrayl set up his private office at the new sanctuary in 1991, he began to seclude himself from the people. No longer did he associate freely with his brothers and sisters—only by appointment did they get to visit with him.

As a gift, the Elders bought Yisrayl a very nice coffee pot. When Yisrayl held appointments on the Sabbaths, with these same Elders, they would be offered a cup of coffee from this appliance. Yisrayl's cup would be filled with coffee and peach brandy, even when he was scheduled to preach that morning.

I did the best that I could. Since Yisrayl and "she" were holed up together, like rats in the office, I became more involved with the people of the congregation. I continued playing the piano and singing in the Choir. I organized the food purchases for the feasts. I made sure that ten issues of The Prophetic Word were ready for publication, and I pasted and numbered the pages of the books to which they would be converted. I attended all events and parties. I had so many things to do. The growth of the congregation continued unabated.

I had also outgrown him, the corn-fed cowboy with the weak chin and Stetson hat. Even though he had changed his name, and grown a beard, and changed into a dress suit; he had not changed his stripes. Although he put on the façade of Yisrayl Hawkins and perfect righteousness, inside he was still the same old Buffalo Bill Hawkins— the same old man who repeatedly made the same old bad decisions; who continuously committed the same old bad mistakes. He never learned a lesson from his failures, because he never accepted responsibility for them—which might have prevented him from repeating them. Instead, the mistakes that he made were never his fault; he always blamed someone, or something, else.

Margo's Wedding

Since the Feast of Tabernacles and Last Great Day were scheduled from September 24 through October 1, 1991, we scheduled Margo's Wedding for Sabbath evening, September 21, 1991. I organized her wedding while also planning for the feast. Margo's long white wedding dress was beautifully accented with a purple bouquet of flowers. Her bridesmaids were dressed in purple satin. The groom was dressed in a black suit, with a white shirt and purple tie. His tallit and kippah were also white. The groomsmen were also dressed accordingly. Yisrayl performed the ceremony as the couple stood under the canopy. The groom smashed the wineglass into a zillion slivers with the heel of his shoe. This was also a lavish affair. Yisrayl did not say a word about the money that I spent on her, as he usually would have done; "she" was there now to listen to the conversation.

I cannot explain to you how joyous this Feast of Tabernacles was in 1991. The feast keepers registered at the front office when they arrived. Yisrayl had built an office in the front, and behind the office Yisrayl had purchased a nice mobile home in which "she" resided. There was the *Italian Night In* for a spaghetti dinner get-together. There were *what you bring is what we eat* meals. There was an *Israeli Dance night*. There was a talent show. There was a children's show. There were chaperoned Youth Group get-togethers, so our young people could meet and socialize with each other. There were prayer times for the men and women. There was light and gladness everywhere. White-wall tents, mobile homes, and travel trailers were grouped all around the sanctuary. This was wonderful. These beautiful people were my family, just as my own children were.

The Dedication of The House of Yahweh new sanctuary was on Sunday during this feast, on September 29, 1991. The Elders were wearing their new tallits made with white linen trimmed with black and gold stripes, with black linen kippahs on their heads. When they marched by the music into the sanctuary from the east entrance, it was stunning. The sanctuary and the land were dedicated to Yahweh. The Shamarim were standing guard, unarmed.

At that moment I could not see, or maybe I had refused to allow myself to see, how the citizens of the local community could possibly be afraid or suspicious of us. Being a part of such a great family as this, with the love that we had for each other, even caused me to forget my pain and humiliation.

It would only be later, when I was out of this closed community, that I would be able to understand that the people outside of this group were only glaring at the "darkness" which Yisrayl Hawkins was openly portraying to them. Because of his actions, and decisions, they were not able to behold the "light" of Yahweh Himself, which we on the inside were seeing.

1992
Growth, Understanding, and Joy

The "new light" which was given in 1991, about the translation of Isayah 43:28, "...I will dissolve the Levitical Priesthood..." revealed the understanding that "The Firstborn Priesthood" would be reinstated when the Messiah returned.

It was preached that the members of The House of Yahweh could actually attain to the position of "priest" in The New World. With this understanding, it was believed that all of Yahweh's Priestly Laws must be researched, studied and practiced. A section of this law included the "laws of the family purity" found in Leviticus Chapter Twelve and Chapter Fifteen.

The Elders who had been given the responsibility of researching these purity laws were not able to formulate a solid conclusion. Yisrayl Hawkins then gave this responsibility to me.

During the course of this research, Yisrayl Hawkins and I bitterly opposed each other about the interpretation of the scripture written in Exodus 19:15. The Second Printing of *The Book of Yahweh*, 1988 shows,

> And he (Moses) said to the people; Prepare yourselves for the third day. Do not come near your wives.

The Sixth Printing of *The Book of Yahweh*, 1993, shows Yisrayl's personal interpretation of this scripture:

> And he said to the people; Be those who are prepared by the third day, but you may not draw near with the women.

This is a huge difference. Exodus 19:10-11 shows a three day process, culminating with everyone being ready to meet Yahweh on Mount Sinai is the sight of "all" the people; men, women and children. This does not indicate that "men only" were instructed to attend.

I refused to accept Yisrayl's interpretation; women and children were not excluded. Yisrayl refused to accept the correct translation, I later learned, because he had his own agenda. To make a long story short, I simply did not make any reference to Exodus 19:15 when the booklet was written.

At the time I asked myself, "Why would he want to do this?" It would be revealed to me later that Yisrayl was promoting "men only" in his "firstborn priesthood" to appeal to their carnal pride and vanity. This was Yisrayl's first step in order to consolidate his power. Women would have to be reduced to the status of property and things, having no legal right to object to their husband's practice of polygamy. This was not only a "men only" manipulation; it was also a "women-hating" manipulation.

In February, 1992, the booklet about the purity laws was published, and was only available to members of The House of Yahweh. It was my understanding that the focus was now upon attaining to the office of "priest" in the New World, so the potential candidates for this office, both men and women, had to know these laws. The contents of this booklet openly promoted "loving and pure monogamy in marriage."

Yisrayl Hawkins was busy with other things when this booklet was distributed. When he did finally read it, he found there was no reference to Exodus 19:15 and "men only."

He confronted me about this. I told him that I did not need this scripture to finish the booklet, and that I was going to have no part in delegating the women in The House of Yahweh to the status of second class citizens.

The members read this booklet, "The Laws of the Family Purity," and positive spiritual results followed. This was the year that extensive bible studies were conducted. The New World Training Center for men and women focused their studies on the booklets published by The House of Yahweh. The Men's Law Class and the Women's Law Class researched the laws extensively. There were different classes almost every weekday night, centered upon Yahweh only. There were also fun events to raise money for different projects, including a monthly newsletter entitled, "The Reporter." It was always delightful to receive my issue of this newsletter to keep up with the "family news."

There were established House of Yahweh congregations in Trinidad, Nigeria, and Canada at this time, with many other members meeting in informal groups; and all of them were part of my family. A Children's Storybook was in the process of research to publication. There was also a group of Midwives who helped deliver the babies in the congregation.

Yahshua's Memorial and Feast of Passover and Unleavened Bread were set for April 18 through April 25, 1992. This was such a wonderful, spiritual time. Everything was fun, joyous, and exciting and I was involved in almost everything. I remember that I entered a raffle for something, and my name was announced from the pulpit as the winner! I was so excited.

Years later, I found a mundane document in a picture frame in which the glass was broken. When I took this apart to dispose of it, I found a Certificate of Appreciation in Teaching presented to me, Deaconess Kay Hawkins, dated April 22, 1992, during the Feast of Unleavened Bread. This has Yisrayl Hawkins' signature on it, but he never gave this to me. This is typical of his envy and mean spiritedness. He had to be the center of attention in all things, and this certificate was proof to him that he wasn't. Looking back and knowing what I know now, Yisrayl began to see me as a threat to his absolute power, position, and authority. He began to see me as "satan," his adversary.

On Sunday, June 7, 1992, the day before Pentecost, Justin, our youngest son, was married in The House of Yahweh sanctuary in Eula. Again, this was a lavish ceremony with almost all of the members present. I also helped plan the event. Justin and his new wife moved into a mobile home which was set up on our home place. I was glad he lived so close. I was now alone with my work.

It would have been July, 1992, that I had a hysterectomy performed in Hendrick Memorial Hospital. I had not had a physical examination since Justin was born. When I decided that I should, it was discovered that I had Level-4 Dysplasia of the cervix, a pre-cancerous condition, caused by the human papilloma virus. I was anointed by the Elders for healing.

Afterward I told Yisrayl that I was going to have surgery to remove this. When he asked me if I wanted to wait on Yahweh for healing, I couldn't believe what I was hearing. I thought to myself, "What a hypocrite!" I knew that Yisrayl Hawkins didn't hesitate to seek the services of a physician on every occasion that required one, and so would I.

Yahweh had given me enough sense to understand that it was Him who sent me to the female physician in the first place, just in time to be cured by Yahweh as He guided the female surgeon's hands.

The Feast of Tabernacles and Last Great Day were scheduled from October 12 through October 19, 1992. I could hardly wait for the feast to begin; I would soon again be seeing all of my family who lived out of town. Camp sites for tent, campers, and motor-homes had been set up. The services during the feast were scheduled for 10:00 in the morning and 2:30 in the afternoon, with a Hearing Interpreter for the hearing impaired. The Choir sang during every song service; rehearsals were scheduled and auditions were encouraged. There was a General Store, House of Yahweh Restaurant, and a gift shop; my granddaughter bought me a ceramic owl from this gift shop which I still have. Events scheduled during this feast were the *Annual Italian Night In,* the *Family Reunion Night,* during which new babies and new couples were given gift showers. The Men and Women's classes held a Graduation Ceremony, and there was a Variety Show Night; this was so much fun! The Youth Group for our young people ages 12-20 was active and involved; the children who attended public schools received excused absences. There were times for men's prayer and for women's prayer, and on the Last Great Day of the feast there was a buffet Farewell Dinner for everyone.

Each feast was progressively more joyous, exciting, and spiritual than the previous one. Everyone was growing in unity and love for each other, with all purity. I was praying for the day that Yisrayl Hawkins would somehow come out of his spiritual stupor and infatuation with "her," and join me again. I knew that he would lose interest in her eventually, just as he had always done before. I knew this situation would change. I just did not realize at the time that the change would be for the worse—for me, for all the other members, and for the organization of The House of Yahweh itself.

CHAPTER SIXTEEN

1992
Rumors, Paranoia, and Apprehension

The year, 1992, started with Yisrayl becoming more and more paranoid. Over the years he had obsessed about Randy Weaver and the Ruby Ridge incident in Idaho. There was also the bad publicity about the sect leader in Florida who had given himself the name, Yahweh ben Yahweh, which had floated around since the mid 1980s.

By January, 1992, the case against Yahweh ben Yahweh and 15 members of his religious sect, the secretive "Yahweh nation," was scheduled for trial. The article entitled, *Yahweh case moves forward*, was published in the Friday, January 3, 1992, issue of *The Dallas Morning News*, page 4-A, released by *The Associated Press*, These excerpts state,

> If they can indict this religion, they can go after any religion, Mr. Yahweh's defense attorney Alcee Hastings said outside court. The 56-year-old Mr. Yahweh, born Hulon Mitchell Jr. in Enid, Oklahoma faces up to 60 years in prison and $60,000 in fines if convicted of conspiracy to commit 14 murders, two attempted murders, extortion, arson and other violence. ...The judge allowed the defendants to wear their traditional white garments, but he said they can't use their sect names during the trial. He has ruled that Yahweh spectators can't wear their robes, saying it would be as intimidating to the jurors as if sheet-wearing Ku Klux Klan members were in attendance. That

decision has been challenged by the American Civil Liberties Union to the 11th Circuit Court of Appeals in Atlanta on the grounds that it violates the Yahwehs' freedom of religion, ACLU director Robyn Blummer said Thursday. [32]

The shadow of that publicity, according to Yisrayl Hawkins, was darkening the image of our organization. The glib remark that Yisrayl had previously made in 1990, "Rumors Don't Worry The House of Yahweh," was proving to be quite untrue.

Yisrayl Hawkins compulsively followed this case. The two men had so much in common. Yisrayl was 57-years-old in 1992, Mitchell was 56; both of them were associated with "Yahweh." Yisrayl had sold bibles from door to door in Enid, Oklahoma, where Mitchell was born, and his right hand man was a woman, just as was Yisrayl's.

Yisrayl was dealing with rumors concerning guns, just as Hulon Mitchell Jr., and both were presiding over secretive organizations. The greatest fear Yisrayl had was that if the court could indict this "Yahweh group," then they would go after The House of Yahweh. The implications were that the Federal Government would somehow receive the authority to view the organization's financial records, to learn what Yisrayl Hawkins was actually doing with all of the money that was coming in.

Throughout 1992, Yisrayl was also busy putting out various fires and conflicts, in order to consolidate his power and control. He was occupied bringing judgments against some of the members who charged him with indecent behavior with other women. Some of the members were studying together on Friday evenings, with only the head of household teaching the laws of Yahweh. Yisrayl would not allow anyone to "usurp" his authority, so he set out to squash these types of independent gatherings. He began a thought process to bring everyone under his absolute control. Members were given instructions to study The House of Yahweh material, only, and were told not to watch television for entertainment.

An application for a Business and Educational Radio Frequency was sent to the FCC on June 29, 1992. When the equipment was operational,

---

32 Used with permission of The Associated Press Copyright© 2012. All rights reserved.

the congregation was instructed to listen only to The House of Yahweh radio station. Yisrayl Hawkins' sermons blared continuously.

The messages in the sermons now instructed that in order to learn correctly, the members were to ask everything of the Elders. No longer was it "prove the scriptures to see if they were of Yahweh." It was now "believe Yisrayl," a physical man who made many mistakes, and many more bad decisions.

The members were also instructed to believe that their only "family" was members of The House of Yahweh, not their blood relatives.

The pages of The Book of Yahweh were scanned into a computer by Elder David Verner, also known as Elder Yahudah Hawkins, Yisrayl's loyal "research specialist." This made it possible for "corrections" to The House of Yahweh version of the bible to be done secretly, according to Yisrayl Hawkins' express wish and command.

Proverbs 28:1 says that an evil man flees when no one is chasing him. Yisrayl was also afraid that someone was going to kill him. Yisrayl's paranoia led him to take different routes to any destination. He stayed in different places every night. He looked over his shoulder, expecting at any time that a law enforcement officer would be right there to pick him up. He had no peace himself, and therefore gave no peace to those closely associated with him, much less to the members of the congregation. Sermons of "persecution" by the "damnable Christians," and "rumors about The House of Yahweh" flew out of his mouth from the pulpit, aided by several gulps of peach brandy before he appeared on the stage.

Instructions about tent, trailer, and mobile home spaces on The Forty Four being private property were issued, with the instructions that if any outside law officer wanted to inspect their premises they were to refuse permission.

The Feast of Tabernacles and Last Great Day were scheduled from October 12 at sunset through October 19, 1992, at sunset. The days leading up to this feast found Yisrayl Hawkins filled with agitation and apprehension. On October 2, 1992, a rambling letter was created and sent to the American Civil Liberties Union to request that this government entity intervene to allay our fears. Excerpts from a copy of this letter follow,

It does not take much to stir up anger and hatred in a group who is ready to find fault. It also takes VOTES to be re-elected, and the Governing Entities found that "The House of Yahweh" and hatred for us, was a topic that voter and candidate could both "agree."

The letter goes on to relay the events of the Hawkins Subdivision Public Water Facility, which we were still defending and denying at the time. This letter continues,

> The rumors which had previously circulated were: We sacrificed dogs, we do not use soap, we have buried a truck load of automatic weapons on this property, everyone in The House of Yahweh is on food stamps… we are a militant hate group, we barricade all who come here and no one is allowed to leave, we hold members against their will, work them continuously, do not feed them, we are a strange, secretive cult.
>
> Now, we have heard RUMORS, which we feel are valid, that Bill Johnson, the County Judge in Clyde, Texas, will be issuing a SEARCH WARRANT "DURING" the dates established for The Feast of Tabernacles. He is alleged to be issuing it to search for "buried automatic weapons" (and there are none!) or to search for narcotics (and there are none!).
>
> It is our FEAR that once these "Officials" gain access to the Sanctuary Land owned by The House of Yahweh, that they will PLANT narcotics, or DISCOVER automatic weapons. This fear is justified, since Yisrayl Bill Hawkins was once on the Abilene Police Department, and actually saw drugs being planted in residences for which a Search Warrant had been obtained.
>
> We know that we may "sound paranoid", but our fears are very real. In fact, Gary Brown, around the middle of July, 1992, phoned the Office of the FBI because of the rumors about weapons and drugs, and informed them that he, personally, would escort the authorities over every foot of this Sanctuary Property at any time EXCEPT during a religious festival, to show them that these rumors were nothing but vicious lies. Your help or your advice to avoid this confrontation will be forever appreciated. Signed, Yisrayl Hawkins/Mrs. Yisrayl Hawkins

On October 12, 1992, a faxed letter was received from Suzanne Donovan, American Civil Liberties Union of Texas, which stated,

> I'm sorry but there really is nothing the ACLU of Texas could do to help your group avoid a potential confrontation. We can not respond to rumors or hearsay, and can not do anything on a pre-emptive basis in any event. I certainly hope your festival goes smoothly. Unfortunately, the issues you present are not of civil liberties nature.

The Feast of Tabernacles and Last Great Day went smoothly. The Shamarim and members remained on high alert, but there were no confrontations with any law enforcement agencies on the sanctuary property.

CHAPTER SEVENTEEN

1993
The Great Depression

The year, 1993, started well enough. I was busy doing the writing and typesetting; business as usual. It would have been about the middle of February that I learned that Margo's prenatal checkup from the midwife unit did not go well. Something was wrong with my youngest daughter.

Around the first week in March, Margo was in the hospital surrounded by all The House of Yahweh midwives. Margo refused to stay in the hospital to be tested, so she left against physician's advice. She soon returned to the hospital, running a fever and vomiting. I went to visit with her. She was surrounded by so many visitors, including the midwives whom I thought were capable. Yisrayl assured me that she was being well taken care of. She left the hospital again. Margo went into premature labor and delivered a son on March 15, 1993. When I went to the hospital to visit her and the baby, she was in the Intensive Care Unit, battling for her life.

I went to see Margo every day after this, praying for her recovery. I took the baby home with me to care for him, and brought him to see Margo every afternoon. Yisrayl complained to me that I was not doing "Yahweh's work." I informed him that I was doing His work by caring for my daughter and grandson, and if he was inferring that I needed to be at home, doing the writing and typesetting, that he had others who might be able to do this.

I told Yisrayl Hawkins that I was absolutely going to be with my child; that somehow, every time that I did not go to visit Margo, she fell back into some sort of crisis. I remember scheduling feast duties on a notebook and making food purchases by phone as I sat and waited in the visitor's area in the hospital.

Margo endured at least three surgeries to drain all of the infection from her abdomen. She does not remember much about this time period. I remember praying to Yahweh to spare Margo's life, and He sent His messengers: the right surgeon and hospital staff. His hand guided their hands. It was told to me later by another physician that he had only seen three other persons with the same type of peritonitis that Margo had, but all of them had died.

Yahshua's Memorial and Passover Feast of Unleavened Bread were scheduled for April 7 through April 14, 1993. Margo was released from the hospital one day before the feasts began. I was so grateful that she was alive. She was weak and frail as she began attending the services, but she was becoming stronger every day.

The auditorium was almost filled to capacity that spring of 1993. Yahshua's Memorial was observed reverently. The Passover celebration the next night was the most spiritual and exciting event I could ever remember. This was the "ball" of the year and almost everyone was formally dressed. The Seder was read. The dinner was buffet style, with the Elders serving the entrée. The choir sang *The Song of Mosheh,* as well as the song, *Passover Round.*

Each husband sat with his one wife and their children as everyone celebrated together. For the remainder of the feast week, the sermons were inspired. The music was wonderful. The dinners with the out-of-towners were delightful. The Special Sisters group of Elders' wives was so enjoyable. There was always something to do for everyone here, young and old, and it was almost always something fun.

To me, almost everything was perfect. There was still Yisrayl's irresponsible behavior with "her." I kept praying and waiting for Yisrayl to come to his senses in order to understand that what he was doing was absolutely wrong on every level—physically, mentally, and spiritually.

The Bureau of Alcohol and Firearms had launched a raid on the Branch Davidians in Waco, Texas, on February 28, 1993. Four agents and several Branch Davidians died in the shootout. Yisrayl focused his entire time and attention on the events that followed. The previous year the shootout between Federal Agents and Randy Weaver on Ruby Ridge in Idaho had been his center of attention, along with the "Yahweh nation" and Yahweh ben Yahweh.

Yisrayl just knew that the government was out to get him next. Yisrayl moved the printing equipment into storage so it could not be confiscated. He came to the house and took every address that was on file so the names of the members of The House of Yahweh would not be known, or that's what he told me. Every effort was taken to thwart any action. Paranoia and fear seemed to dictate almost his every move.

On April 19, 1993, Federal Agents tried to drive out the Branch Davidians with teargas after a 51-day standoff. As many as 86 members, including David Koresh, the leader, and 24 children, were thought to have died as the flames raced through the wooden buildings. The headline on the Tuesday, April 20, 1993, edition of *The Abilene Reporter News* said it all, *"Inferno Devours Cult."*

When Yisrayl becomes agitated about anything, he becomes extremely short tempered and violent. He screams at those close to him, and hurts everyone's feelings without a second thought. I was glad that I was not around Yisrayl Hawkins when the Branch Davidians and their buildings went up in fire.

It was at 5:05 pm on Tuesday, May 18, 1993, that the phone rang. When I answered, it was "her," crying. I sensed immediately that she and Yisrayl were fighting about something. Whimpering, she said, "Kay, I know you don't know it, but I'm Yisrayl's wife."

I said, "Yisrayl's wife? What makes you think that you are his wife?" She stated, "Because of our marriage vows."

Rage is the emotion I remember most. When I hung up the phone, I got the keys to my car and drove out to Lake Fort Phantom Hill where Yisrayl was hiding out. He was sitting in his office when I arrived and was surprised to see me. "She" was not there. I called him every name in the book but a white man. I then got back into my car and drove to Abilene to the sanctuary grounds. I got out of my car, walked up the steps to the door of her mobile home, and knocked. I remember there was a sign on the door, "Do not knock. Knocks will not be answered." "She" answered and let me in.

I had never before been in her dwelling. It was very nice. I could see that it was well appointed with new furniture. It was determined that Elder David Verner had officiated at their "wedding ceremony." She would not tell me the date that it was performed. I was only in her living room for a few minutes before Yisrayl arrived and opened the door, without knocking.

When he was standing there it was all I had in me to remain somewhat composed. I would have preferred to have scratched both of their eyes out, Yisrayl's first, but I did not become physically violent. I told "her," "I know this man, and I know that it would be best if you would buy a piece of property in your own name, and move your mobile home onto it. I know that if you don't, one of these days you will have nothing left but the clothes on your back."

I left them standing there, together. I went to my car and drove home, crying all the way.

I waited for Yisrayl to call me, which would have been about 8:00 that evening. I begged Yisrayl to come home to me. He said to me, "I won't be a dog on a chain."

I again told Yisrayl that what he had done was actually to have committed adultery, and if he did not repent of this that it would destroy him and The House of Yahweh. He answered me with the most calm, self-righteous, arrogant voice that I had ever heard, "I have not sinned."

I was waiting for an apology and works of repentance. What I got was an insult and a slap in the face.

When rage is not released, it turns inward into depression. All of those times that I had defended him from gossip about other women came to mind. When Yisrayl had told me, "I will not sin," what he actually meant was, "When I am doing this, I am not sinning."

I dropped into the blackest mental hole of pain and was on the verge of a mental breakdown. I did not know that such a burden could exist. It did not help that the Feast of Pentecost would be observed in less than ten more days. I was praying constantly that Yahweh would cause Yisrayl to change his mind and turn away from this.

When Buffalo Bill Hawkins changed his name to "Yisrayl," he proclaimed that this name meant, "He will rule as Yahweh." Again, every Hebrew word has a meaning. *"Yisrael,"* according to *Strong's*

Exhaustive Concordance, Hebrew Dictionary, means, *"He will rule as God."* According to cult lingo, "the God of this world is Satan."

As I listened to Yisrayl's sermons during this Feast of Pentecost, I knew from his message that he had become set upon his own agenda. He was not going to repent, because "he had not sinned." He was going to "keep every law," and he was going to make sure that the taking of multiple wives was part of it.

Yisrayl made it his business to know what was going on in the organization. He knew that some men had a problem with lusting after women other than their own wife, but he also knew these same men had kept their hands to themselves to this point. These were the men he initially manipulated.

The first time a married man specifically brought along an unmarried woman with him to one of the meetings was on a Sabbath in June, 1993. He made it quite clear that he was there with his wife, and also his girlfriend. It was scandalous. Gossip was flying everywhere about it.

That night an Elder's meeting was scheduled. This man's wife brought her grievance about her husband's indecent behavior with this other woman to the Judges, the Elders. It was Yisrayl who told her that she was wrong, and her husband could do whatever he wanted. She was to shut up and accept it.

I saw what was happening. Yisrayl manipulated every movement that had taken place, beginning with the man bringing his girlfriend to services. Yisrayl is a coward and would not take the lead to initiate multiple marriages himself, so he was manipulating others to cut the path. I told Yisrayl, "You're determined to push this, aren't you?" Paul Schneider, also known as Shaul Schneider, Shaul Hawkins, or even Yisrayl Hawkins as far as I know, said to me, "You seem upset." Yes, I was.

The scriptures say not to involve the "little ones" in something which would destroy their faith. So, the following Monday I went to visit Elder Shaul Schneider at this place of work. I told Shaul what Yisrayl had done behind my back: that "she" had told me on May 18th that she was Yisrayl's wife, and that I was worried that this would destroy The House of Yahweh. Shaul seemed shocked. I also told Shaul that Yisrayl took married women in the congregation to his hideaways so they could cook and clean for him.

I asked Shaul to investigate and set a panel of Judges to judge between me and Yisrayl Hawkins on this matter; literally, a matter of life or death. If a panel of Judges had been promptly convened to hear my case, then the Elders, the Judges, would have been required to choose between the organization, The House of Yahweh; or the man, Yisrayl Bill Hawkins.

Shaul did speak to Yisrayl about this matter. It was then that Yisrayl probably asked him, "What do you want?"

After our divorce, when I was cleaning out one of my desks, I found a letter to: "Yisrayl, Information You Requested from Shaul and Riyyah." This letter is dated July 4, 1993, hand-written by Shaul Schneider,

> Yisrayl,
>
> In order to pay the rent and meet our other expenses I would need to make $200 per week with Riyyah making $90 a week. Without rent we can get by with me making $160 and week and Riyyah making $90.
>
> Yisrayl, I really do want to devote all my time to this Law Commentary. I only fear being a financial burden on Yahweh's House.
>
> Also, with this wage the only extra help that would be foreseeable would be with major repairs on the car.
>
> Love in Yahshua's Name. Signed, Shaul S.

Shaul Schneider was bribed! A bribe blinds the eyes of those who should see! Yisrayl Hawkins made sure that Elder Shaul Schneider would see things his way, only.

Yisrayl also assigned Shaul to be my "counselor." Yisrayl Hawkins made sure that Elder Shaul Schneider would suppress every cause that I had against him!

There was never a judgment between me and Yisrayl Hawkins by the Judges of The House of Yahweh. Yisrayl certainly did not want me to reveal everything that I knew about him to impartial Judges—who could have saved the organization of The House of Yahweh!

Yisrayl Hawkins and Shaul Schneider made quite sure this would never take place.

Shaul did, however, make sure that the married women who once went to cook and clean for Yisrayl at his hideouts did not continue to do so.

I was sick with grief and depression by this time, and thought that if I changed my name that I could change my thinking. I took the name, "Kallahyah," on June 12, 1993, which means "Yahweh is making perfect, to create a bride for His Son."

During one of his "counseling" sessions, Shaul gave me a book to read. He "counseled" me that I could make myself believe anything by using the instructions written in this book. I thought to myself, "Did I really hear this? Is this what Shaul had already done?"

What I did not know at the time, which I do know now, was that Shaul was attempting to control my mind in order to shut my mouth; projects that would have pleased Yisrayl Hawkins, had they succeeded.

I had one hope remaining. There is absolutely no "law" in the scriptures that states "you may, can, must" take more than one wife. I was praying that Yisrayl would see that he had no scriptural authority for this notion and turn from it.

I stated to Yisrayl that there was no "law" that authorized him to take more than one wife. After this, Yisrayl stayed away from me, and he and his "loyal researchers," "her" included, focused their time and energy studying The Book of Mormon and other polygamous literature in order to refute my statement.

While Yisrayl had hidden himself from me, it became my responsibility to communicate with the Appraisal District of Callahan County about the Tax Exempt Status Request for The House of Yahweh property in Eula, Texas.

It was on December 25, 1992, that in my official capacity as Corporate Secretary for The House of Yahweh, that I wrote a letter to the Appraisal Office in Baird, Texas, to make formal request that the Lands and Property deeded over to The House of Yahweh—by Yisrayl and Kay Hawkins—be granted Tax Exempt Status for the year 1993.

I had called the county appraiser on May 27, 1992, to request Tax Exempt Status for this property in that year, 1992, but was advised that the cut-off date for filing had already passed. I was advised that I could plead extenuating circumstances for failing to meet this deadline, but declined. Taxes were paid for 1992 on The Forty Four, 5 acres which abutted Oak Forest Road, from which the Sanctuary Entrance was carved out, and 1.25 Acres on Highway 603 in Eula, upon which set two brick veneer buildings and one classroom mobile home for the Yliyah School.

On June 16, 1993, in my capacity as Corporate Secretary, I filed twenty-six pages of the Application for Religious Organization Property Tax Exemption for 1993. The Tax Appraiser then began to question the tax exempt status for all the property. It was on June 24, 1993, that I filed a Formal Letter of Protest about this decision.

Just about the time that I put this letter in the mail, I received another one from the Internal Revenue Service, dated June 18, 1993. This stated that our personal income tax records were being examined for the year 1990. Our Audit was scheduled for Monday, July 19, 1993.

At the first of this year I had battled by the side of Margo for her life, which began to mentally exhaust me. Then I was hit between the eyes with Yisrayl and "her" and their "marriage," which drove me into the pit of utter depression. I completed all of the pages for the tax exemption for The House of Yahweh while in this mental state, and now this. How much more could I endure? I was mentally beaten down by this time, but I knew that I needed to pull myself together and begin to fight this as well.

I called our Tax Lady in Abilene who agreed to help us. I then became focused upon putting together the documents that were needed to absolve us of any wrong doing, and thereby save The House of Yahweh.

Yisrayl went with our Tax Lady to the IRS Audit on July 19. She said the Internal Revenue Agent looked over my records and could find no material changes in the tax that we had reported for the years 1990, 1991, and 1992. We were free! The government could not bring us down personally in order to get to The House of Yahweh. We received the official IRS Letter with this determination, dated November 29, 1993.

The Spiritual Death
of The House of Yahweh, Abilene

The moment Yisrayl Hawkins learned that his personal secretary had informed me that they were "married," he had two choices before him. He could have repented of his behavior, turned from it, and saved The House of Yahweh from spiritual destruction. Instead, he became focused upon consolidating absolute power and control, and holding on to his position with a death-grip. He thought only of himself. Remember, nothing is his fault; he did not commit any sin.

He also became focused upon destroying any influence I may have had. Shaul was certainly not successful in his attempts at "mind control." I wouldn't "just believe anything." I wouldn't accept polygamy as a "law" in The House of Yahweh, and I wouldn't stop speaking against it.

From the day that "she" had announced herself as Yisrayl's wife, May 18, 1993—it would take over two months for Yisrayl to "create" a sermon which would be brought over the pulpit of The House of Yahweh. Mistranslated scriptures would be combined, and presented as "proof" for a law that did not exist.

It would not be until July 24, 1993, that another Elder, Kepha Arcemont, would be given the duty of presenting the "law" of "multiple wives" to the congregation.

The scripture in Exodus 21:10 would be misinterpreted to mean that a man should not deprive his <u>first wife</u> of food, clothing, and marital rights <u>"when" he took another wife</u>.

This misinterpretation was immediately followed by only these words, written in Deuteronomy 27:26, "…Cursed is the one who does not <u>uphold every word of this Law, by carrying it out</u>…"

Kepha finished his sermon by stating that the men in the congregation could take more than one wife, and this was "The Law."

Never before had anyone intentionally "twisted" the scriptures over the pulpit in The House of Yahweh, but it was done on this day.

You could hear a pin drop for about two seconds. A woman in the back of the congregation shouted, "That's not right!" I immediately went to Kepha and said, "Yisrayl gave this to you, didn't he!?"

I then revealed to Kepha the events that had transpired since May 18, and that Yisrayl wanted to cover up his sin rather than repent of it.

I also told Kepha there was no "law" granting men the right to more than one wife.

Kepha also went to Yisrayl about this. Kepha then got what he wanted all along—a second, young and pretty, wife.

The next item on Yisrayl's agenda was to preside over a Men's Law Class which would mark me for the remainder of the time that I was in The House of Yahweh: I had to be demoralized, demonized, and branded as a "law hater."

The worst thing that can happen to anyone in The House of Yahweh is for someone to "lose their understanding." This is exactly what Yisrayl insinuated about me; he took premeditated steps to libel and slander me to the whole congregation; he set out to destroy me, in order to destroy any influence that I might have had.

The Men's Law Class was the first place he started. On Tuesday evening, August 17, 1993, Yisrayl Hawkins taped the session. The next night this tape was played during the Women's Law Class. Yisrayl made sure that I was not present to hear it.

It was afterward ordered to be destroyed so that I might not hear it, nor could anyone else know of its existence. One of the men in the sound room made a copy of it and gave it to my son, Justin, who gave it to me.

I could not listen to it in its entirety when I first received it. It was so emotionally painful to hear my own husband slandering and lying about me.

It was not until the year 2005 that I was finally mentally able to transcribe this tape. Yisrayl Hawkins made these statements,

> But when I saw that somebody was stumbling over this…I got to thinking of all these scriptures that…and the most horrible thought, I guess that I've ever had in my life entered my mind, you know, uh, that you know, maybe even my own wife…would not make it because they would want to reject one of Yahweh's Laws or not uphold one of Yahweh's Laws….I heard of wives…crying about it and not accepting it, or didn't want it to be a part of their life…I had it in my own life…I mean my wife…didn't accept this with gladness either. And uh, uh, but I, I keep praying that she will. But she didn't.

Yisrayl then quoted Romans 13:1-2, beginning with "Let every person be subject to the governing authorities…"

> …here we have in our own family someone who, you know, just suddenly goes crazy; and they blame the Law of Yahweh… You will have salvation if you remain in The Faith, in the "authorities" that I have placed…
>
> You know, if somebody wanted to get married to a second wife tonight or tomorrow, I would certainly uphold it…if my wife died right now…I probably would never, ever marry again… there's no way that I would ever want to break in somebody else…my wife is probably the most hateful woman on the face of the earth when Satan's got hold of her mind…I don't thank (sic) your wife is nearly as bad as mine. Ha, ha, ha, ha, ha.

I was marked as a law-hating heretic who had lost all of her understanding. Thereafter, my every effort to prevent the evil that was engulfing The House of Yahweh was looked upon as the pathetic antics of a "mad woman," but this didn't keep me from trying.

I was advised by Elder Walter Jandrisevits that, "Yisrayl will crush you." I thought to myself, "Not if Yahweh has anything to do with it."

Every Sabbath after July 24 one young, deceived Elder after another preached about the "beauty" of this "law," that the Mormons loved this law because they practiced it, that this "law" would be practiced in the world to come, etc. etc. etc. The scriptures were rewritten in I Timothy 3:2, I Timothy 3:12, and Titus 1:6 to state that the word, "one" was now to be translated as "unity." The "husband of one wife" was now to become "in unity as husband and wife."

There was nothing else to talk about but "upholding this law." These sermons hurt my spirit so much that as soon as I finished playing the piano for the opening song service, I would get up and leave. I would study in my feast trailer until about the time for the closing song service, when I would return to play the piano. The words of the songs in The House of Yahweh songbook, *The Songs of Praise to Yahweh,* had not become defiled.

The Feast of Tabernacles this year was from October 2 through October 9, 1993. The days were filled with sermons and joyous events.

My heart was very heavy. I could barely enjoy anything but my children and grandchildren. During my free time, I would cook dinners and invite my children in the evenings for food and fellowship.

It was the Third Day of the Feast, Monday, October 4, 1993, in the evening that the annual *Italian Night In* was scheduled. Yisrayl told me to meet him in his office and we would go to this event together. When I arrived, he was dressed but said he had something else to do first. About a moment later "she" walked in, dressed to attend this event.

I immediately knew what Yisrayl had planned to do—he wanted to walk out into the dining area in the sanctuary, with me on one arm and "her" on his other—his own two wives together with him.

There was simply no way that I was going to validate or approve of his "marriage" to "her." I said to Yisrayl, "What's she doing here?" "She" is going with us," he stated. I said, "I don't care what you two do together, but I'm not going to do this."

I walked to the door by myself, opened it, and went to sit down by Gene and Dottie at their table in the auditorium. As I was conversing with this Elder and his wife, Yisrayl and "she" slinked up and sat down together, directly across from me. I said to Yisrayl, "You can sit here by yourself with "her," I'm having no part of this." I got up, and left them to each other.

I walked over to the table where my children were sitting, where I began enjoying myself. My children bought me about 30 plastic roses that night—souvenirs purchased during the *Italian Night In*. I still have some of them, arranged attractively in one of my vases.

A little while later Yisrayl skulked over, without "her," and angrily sat down beside me; his plot had failed. I did not say a word to him.

A tiger does not change his stripes, and Yisrayl Hawkins could not change the same con-artist ploy that he had pulled on me so many years ago. Remember, he had taken "me" out on my birthday, but it turned out to be "me and her?" His manipulation did not work the second time.

This same night, October 4, 1993, Justin's wife delivered their baby son. It was a difficult delivery, natural childbirth. I held my grandson the next morning. He was over 22 inches long and weighed over 9 pounds. I experienced a roller coaster of emotions within twenty-four hours; wrenching agony and wonderful delight.

Yisrayl and his current tactics of libel, slander, and deception were not working on me; I was still not accepting "his law" of multiple wives. Extreme measures were now going to be taken, and the hammer came down from the pulpit, pounding "authority and headship" in The House of Yahweh—who is your authority and you must submit to Yahweh's authorities.

Looking back, and knowing what I know now, Yisrayl Hawkins was a lying hypocrite when he proclaimed that he was one of "Yahweh's authorities." Remember, he would not submit to Jacob's "authority and headship," when Jacob Hawkins ordained him as an Elder in The House of Yahweh, Odessa, in 1980?

Nevertheless, sermon after sermon was now focused on authority and submission. I was not impressed with the topic. I advised Yisrayl that if he behaved like the Messiah, there would not be a problem.

My actions were duly noted, so Yisrayl arranged for four of his loyal Elders and their wives to come to see me. They know who they are. They did not want to hear what I had to say. They wanted Yisrayl to hear them tell me that I was not accepting Yisrayl's authority over me as my head, and it was me who was the sinner, not him.

I was sitting at my place at my dining room table. Yisrayl was sitting at the head. I stood up and pointed my finger at them, waving an arc to encompass all of them, and said, "You are all nothing but a bunch of pimps and whores. Get out of my house!"

Yisrayl stepped into the living room and turned on his crocodile tears; Ana went over to pet him. They left. I asked Yisrayl what he thought that he had accomplished with this spectacle. The crocodile tears immediately ceased and the blank, glazed, faraway stare took their place.

Years later, I learned that this was a typical con-act put on by people like Yisrayl Hawkins. The others could not understand that Yisrayl had manipulated them to view him as "wounded, in emotional pain, and suffering," while they viewed me as "rebellious and hateful."

This was the first of the onslaughts, like waves that keep washing up and rolling back. I was condemned. It was me who was the sinner. I had lost it. What is all the fuss about? Almost every Elder, and some of the women, had taken a punch at me. Yet, Yisrayl insisted that I continue to write *The Prophetic Word* during this whole time. I had not lost enough of my understanding to prevent this.

The pressure to conform to this evil was overwhelming. One day I told Yisrayl that I was going to my feast trailer to fast and pray. I let myself in with my own key. When I walked by Yisrayl's office, I saw a stack of $20 dollar bills lying on the floor, which was about an inch thick. I picked up the pile and set it on his desk.

As I was studying the next afternoon, there was a knock on the door. When I answered, there stood Elder Yaaqob Mosheh, known previously as Elder J.E. Martin, with his wife, Elder Kepha Arcemont with his wife, and Elder Yeremyah Jeffries with his wife.

They were sent by Yisrayl to oppose and condemn me. Mosheh had two small pebbles in his hand. When he sat down in one of my chairs, he threw them at me, and stated that Yahweh could raise up writers in The House of Yahweh with these stones. I very quietly stooped down and picked these up. One is white, the other black. I still have them.

I proceeded to inform Mosheh that he was misinformed about many things. I also stated to Yeremyah that I had no proof, but that I was of the opinion that his wife and Yisrayl had something going on between them. This gave them something else to think about.

The next day, when Yisrayl came home, I threw the pile of $20 dollar bills in his face. I advised him that I was not tempted by filthy lucre, as was he, and that I was not a thief.

This was how I learned Yisrayl's method of entrapment, and this is the information that Yahweh wanted me to have when my fasting and prayer was over—that Yisrayl was the one who planted the bait in order to destroy someone, and if they took it, he, or she, was condemned in a smear campaign and driven out of The House of Yahweh.

I remembered the many others who had been accused of theft by Yisrayl Hawkins—his little secretary before "her" among them. I thought to myself, "So this was how his sweet little secretary had been framed, so she could be gotten rid of so conveniently."

Yisrayl only thought of himself, and what he wanted. He didn't care about anyone else or their eternal life.

It was on Sabbath, November 20, 1993, that Yisrayl Hawkins informed the congregation that "all responsibility" was taken from the people, from Deacons on down, and the "Body of Elders" were completely responsible for everything. No longer was it "study to show yourself approved;" it was now "obey the Elders," whatever it was that Yisrayl told them to say.

The Holy Scriptures meant nothing. They were only something to rewrite and add-to, in order to make them fit Yisrayl's own demented notions.

The next Sabbath, Elder David Verner (Elder Yahudah Hawkins) brought a sermon entitled, "Put out the Leprous, Law #31."

I knew that my days were numbered, but I was determined to sit in the sanctuary and watch this organization fall down around my ears. I was not going to leave voluntarily.

About this time Yisrayl began to harp about "vows to Yahweh." I reminded Yisrayl and Shaul Schneider about Yisrayl's wedding vows to me, which were vowed in the Name of Yahweh at the time of the ceremony. I was denounced by both of them, and was informed that they were not valid.

Later I found another document regarding "vows" in The House of Yahweh. This was signed on November 14, 1993, by a woman who was separating herself and her children from her husband. This letter states,

> Ylisha…has physically beaten me on several occasions, and my child on at least one occasion. His abuse has continued for approximately two years to this date. I have prayed for Ylisha and have tried to be humble and submissive so as not to upset his temper. However it has come to the point where I fear for my own and my children's safety.
>
> I refuse to dwell with the violence any longer. He has shown no regard to my physical and mental well-being, nor that of my children's. Before Samuyl's birth, I was admitted to the hospital with a concussion while I was yet pregnant. Yet I was still sent back to live with the man who abused me, with the counselors saying that "Yahweh hates separation," but not under all circumstances. I have determined in my heart that I will no longer live with this "way of Cain," hatred and law-breaking, and as a responsible and loving mother neither will I allow my children to be put through this.
>
> Ylisha, willingly and of his own accord made vows to me and

Yahweh that he would "never strike me again." My counselors set a judgment against him were he to ever break these vows. Their judgment was that "he was to be cast out of The House of Yahweh." Ylisha has repeatedly broken these vows, and yet no consequences were ever pronounced against him.

Scripture tells us that a man shall not be a striker…yet his actions have not been punished. Therefore, I now take the step which Yahweh permits me to take according to I Corinthians 7:10-11, "…a wife must not separate from her husband. But if she does, she must remain unmarried, or else be reconciled to her husband…"

I will follow these dictates and not remarry. I will return to Ylisha when, and only when, he has completed all requirements according to the clauses on the following contract…

The clauses were written on the second page, and this woman signed and dated this document. However, this document is not signed by her husband, Ylisha, or by any of the counselors. Nothing was resolved in her appeal for help.

By this time I had stopped playing the piano for the song services, and had stopped sitting on the front row next to "her". She sat there by herself. I had started sitting with my children in the middle of the crowd. When the sermons started, I would begin playing with my grandchildren so I wouldn't have to pay any attention to them. The only peace that I received was when I was with my children.

Almost every Elder and his wife had turned against me. They believed in Yisrayl Hawkins and refused to believe that he could be wrong in any way whatsoever.

In order to try to get some peace with the situation, on December 11, 1993, I wrote Yisrayl Hawkins a letter in which I said,

Today I make a vow to myself and to Yahweh that I will come under your control and authority. I will do whatever you tell me to do, regardless of my "feelings." I will not run you down, nor will I allow anyone else to run you down, just as I did in the past. I want some "PEACE" IN MY LIFE, and I know that this is the ONLY WAY that I can have it…

This was my exact intention the day that I wrote this. I was on the verge of being spiritually broken. There is a scripture in Numbers 30:5, which refers to a woman living in her Father's House who vows a vow to Yahweh, or vows an oath to bind herself to some pledge:

> But if her Father forbids her when He hears about it, none of her vows or pledges, by which she obligated herself, will stand. Yahweh will release her because her Father has forbidden her.

It was toward the end of December, 1993, that Elder Yeremyah Jeffries installed a septic system and constructed a mobile home pad about the distance of a city block east of my house in Eula. DeeDee's mobile home would be moved here in January, 1994. She and Justin would be close to me in everything that took place from this point forward.

CHAPTER EIGHTEEN

1994

Drama, Divorce, Excommunication

I was becoming sick and tired of being depressed and crying all of the time. I wanted some relief. I heard that one of the women had recently started taking an antidepressant and was feeling much better. Around the first of January, 1994, I made an appointment with her doctor. I made up a story about the cause of my depression, saying that I felt depressed because all of my children had left home. I certainly did not want to tell him the real story. He would have thought that I was crazy, not depressed. I was given a prescription for ten pills, and told to make another appointment for follow-up.

On the next visit I received a thirty-day prescription. I was taking one tablet a day. I started feeling a little better at the end of the second week. By the beginning of February, 1994, I was feeling almost like my old self. I would not be broken or crushed. I was getting mentally stronger every day.

The stronger I became mentally, the less I spoke to Yisrayl Hawkins. I also no longer tried to prove him wrong. Soon he had nothing to rant about from the pulpit; he had no more material. During one of the few times that I did speak to him, he told me that I should submit to his authority and begin to choose his wives for him.

The feasts of Yahshua's Memorial and Yahweh's Passover and Feast of Unleavened Bread were scheduled for March 27 through April 3, 1994. I became busy preparing myself, my home, and the sanctuary for the celebrations. Again, I scheduled the food deliveries. I can say this was not a spiritually satisfying time in my life. During the Passover Celebration, "she" sat with the Elder's wives.

I decided that I also needed some new living room furniture. The couches that I had were bought in 1978, so they were sixteen years old. With our Sears credit card, I purchased three couches. When they were being unloaded by the delivery-men, Yisrayl drove up and came into the house. "What are these?" he asked. I said, "My new furniture." If I was going to live in this house, I should have some new furniture in the living room.

I don't know the moment that I decided to take possession of the things that mattered the most in this world to Yisrayl Hawkins, but I do know the time. Right after the Feast of Unleavened Bread, I decided to take possession of our locked safes and letter files.

I rented a storage place in Abilene. One of the safes and one of the letter files were in my home, and one of each were also in our feast trailer on The Forty Four. I was going to wait until night to take the safe and letter file in my trailer on the feast grounds, but DeeDee said, "No, we are going during the day so it will not look suspicious. We are not stealing. These are yours also."

I had already decided to divorce Yisrayl Hawkins; it was just a matter of time. Prior to this our personal bank account, which had been over $60,000.00, had dwindled to almost nothing. Yisrayl continuously wrote checks for large amounts, but did not make deposits for the same.

I had a stack of receipts written by "her" showing that Yisrayl had made tithe offerings in the amount $300 to $350 every few days. This meant that every few days Yisrayl Hawkins was taking $3000.00 to $3500.00 from The House of Yahweh funds, and I didn't receive any of it.

I knew that I needed some money to combat him and his henchmen when the time came.

There was another motive as well. I wanted all of these young, deceived, impoverished, so-called Elders, who worked for him for almost nothing, to question the reason that he had all of this hidden in the first place.

The next thing I did was to go into Yisrayl's office in our home and open his locked desk. There I found $27,000.00 in cash, a few gold coins, and some silver. I also found a letter to me from Yisrayl, dated February 24, 1987, in which he wrote:

> ...The work that has been started here is the greatest thing on earth at this time. Please do your best to continue it...
>
> You must be strong & become overseer of this work. Do not trust anyone. Prove everything that is done & do not put yourself in a possision (sic) where anyone else will have any power over you. This could cause harm to come to The House of Yahweh.
>
> I know you are honest, I know the work of Yahweh is emportant (sic) to you. That is why I am asking you to stay in charge of all finances. I do not want any money grabbers (sic) to defile the work of Yahweh, and if you stay in charge, handling all finances, it will not occur...
>
> ....go through this desk thoroughly.

I, along with DeeDee and Justin, took the four locked safes and letter files and put them in storage, with my valuable personal records. Looking back, and knowing what I know now, I should have taken these locked safes and letter files directly to my Divorce Attorney. He would have obtained the services of a locksmith, and would have taken a detailed inventory of the contents. I would have received one-half in my divorce, since Texas is a Community Property State. But I didn't.

At the same time that I decided to take possession of the safes and letter files, I began to write a book to refute Yisrayl Hawkins' notions and teachings about "multiple wives."

On April 26, 1994, I received a letter in my mailbox, handwritten by Yisrayl Hawkins. Excerpts from this letter state,

> My dear wife
> Sence (sic) I can't talk to you anymore, without getting upset from the sarcasm I hear in your voice & accusations you contenuelly (sic) make against the Elders, I thought I would write this letter & try to explain my possision (sic)...
> If it were a matter of chooseing (sic) you over another

woman, if it were as simple as that, I would have no trouble at all. But its (sic) much more than that.

...I know that you don't reilize (sic) what you are wanting of me. But the fact is you are asking me to go against what I know is righteous understanding from Yahweh...

...In fact I know of nothing that will turn me or make me relent...

Now I may not be able to convence (sic) you of this, but the point is, I am convenced (sic). And I am going to stake my life on preaching & performing Yahweh's laws...

If falling away takes place, others will be chosen to take their place & carry on the work of exposeing (sic) the Gods & their foolish laws.

But mama if you can get Yahweh to give you back your understanding, you could be a big help in this work and be used clear to the end...

I even know from prophecy that the multipal (sic) wife law will be the deciding factor in keeping some from going to Israyl (sic) after my death...

And why would anyone turn to a sin like gossip, just because they do not understand a law yet?...

Yet they will condem (sic) laws of marrage (sic), that they don't know, because they have never tried them & will not lisson (sic) to the authority Yahweh places over them, to give them understanding.

We have been working long hours to write these laws on marrage (sic) & slavery. We are trying to cover every point so everyone will have all their questions answered.

I pray that you will study it & I pray that you will soon be back on my side doing Yahweh's last days work. Yahweh's Will, will be done.

True love in Yahweh's Name through Yahshua. Y.H.

My position was, "I don't care what you think anymore." On April 29, 1994, Yisrayl left another note,

I am at the 44, call if you want me home...

I did not call. I did not want to see his dirty face. He attributed my new-found resolve and strength to that of finding another man. I was followed everywhere I went so I could be caught in the act. That was pointless, since there was no other physical man.

Yisrayl and four other persons were working on the book entitled, *Reconsidering Yahweh's Laws of Slavery and Marriage Obligations*. This book contains 492 pages which repeatedly state that slavery is good, and that the scriptures do not condemn any man for having more than one wife. The "law" is that if a man takes another wife he must not deprive his first wife of food, clothing, and marital rights, and that this law must be upheld.

The book that I was working on at the same time was entitled, *Marriage In The Plan of Yahweh From The Beginning*, which was completed on April 28, 1994. This book contained 241 pages. As soon as this book was ready, I only made enough copies to give to every Elder.

I requested a Judgment between me and Yisrayl Hawkins. I requested that I be proven wrong in the things written therein.

As soon as the Elders received their copy, the majority of them turned these books over to Yisrayl Hawkins, without reading them. They behaved dutifully, proving they were a bunch of puppets dancing on a string for Yisrayl Hawkins. I received a note from him on May 6, 1994,

> Please don't make matters wors (sic). Give me time to prove
> to you where you are wrong & show you the beauty of Yahweh's
> laws. They all show great love. I have it written. It will soon be in
> your hands. I miss you sweetheart more than I have ever missed
> anything in my life. Love, true love, Y.H.

Another letter went out from Yisrayl telling the Elders to read his book and accept it, and to find fault with the book that I wrote. The fault-finding was entitled, *Grasping at Straws*. Excerpts from the cover-letter, sent with *Grasping at Straws,* state,

To Yahweh's Chosen Elders;
    By now you should have gotten two books, from The House of Yahweh in Abilene...In our book *Yahweh's Laws on Slavery*

and Marriage, full scriptural proof is given. Scriptural proof should be what each Elder bases his life upon.

In the second book, written in opposition to the Scriptures, even the authors admits (sic) that Yahweh's Laws teach slavery and multiple marriage. Christian interpretation is used to condemn Yahweh's Laws in order to cut you off from Yahweh, by persuading you not to uphold Yahweh's words.

Part One, Page 3, of the fault finding, *Grasping at Straws*, states,

Each of the Elders has now in their possession, a draft copy of the TRUE DOCTRINE of The House of Yahweh which is entitled, *Yahweh's Laws on Slavery and Marriage.* The fact that Yahweh shows us in His Inspired, Holy Scriptures that He permits Polygamy, PROVE that Polygamy is an essential part of Yahweh's Perfect Plan and Righteous Pattern of Government from the beginning...

The same thing was happening in The House of Yahweh that happened to The Worldwide Church of God just before I had left that organization. No longer were there sermons in praise of our Heavenly Father. There was only praise for Yisrayl Hawkins, the Anointed One, and the so-called Elders who were controlled by him.

The way of life that I had known for years was over. I had failed my physical family, my own children, and I had also failed my spiritual family, which was the whole congregation of The House of Yahweh. I had failed to prevent Yisrayl Hawkins from falling away from The Faith. No longer would there be light and gladness, joy and peace. The House of Yahweh would cease to grow from within through our sons and daughters each finding their mate and raising their own small, joyous family together.

Satan had been invited in and had completely taken control of Yisrayl Hawkins' thoughts and actions. There was no doubt in my mind that Yahweh had abandoned The House of Yahweh; He had absolutely left the premises.

I did not hear another word from Yisrayl until late in the afternoon on Thursday, May 12, 1994,

Where are the safes? Where did you put them? You are stealing from Yahweh!

I knew that he loved money and power more than anything, and now he didn't have possession of some of the money. The next day, May 13, 1994, I received a Judgment and Decision from the Body of Elders of The House of Yahweh, stating that I was barred from The House of Yahweh and all House of Yahweh property from this date 5-13-94, until I met the following conditions:

1. You are to submit to Yahweh and His Laws by submitting in all things to your lawful head and husband, Elder Yisrayl Hawkins. You are to repent of your rebellion against, and your rejection of his lawful authority over you. You are guilty of rejecting Elder Yisrayl Hawkins' headship over you, and in doing so, you have rejected Yahweh and Yahshua.

     Unless you repent of this sin, you have no hope whatsoever of salvation. Not only have you rejected your husband, but you have rejected the Anointed Servant of Yahweh.

2. You are to no longer teach against the doctrines of The House of Yahweh, that is, the Laws of Yahweh. You are to repent of your action of writing a book which CONDEMNS the Laws of Yahweh as taught by The House of Yahweh to be a doctrine of demons.

3. You are to stop setting yourself, and promoting yourself as a "priest" and a "teacher" of the WHOLE House of Yahweh. This violates the commands of Yahweh as written by the Apostle Shaul. You are neither a "priest" nor a "teacher" of men, and you have no authority whatsoever to do this.

4. You are to stop teaching by going from house to house, either in person, by telephone, or in writing. You are guilty of attempting to turn others away from The House of Yahweh.

5. You must also return the following items that were taken by you without permission or consent from the "House of Yahweh mobile home" used by Elder Yisrayl Hawkins as a Feast Dwelling (located on The House of Yahweh sanctuary grounds).

   A. The safe and all of its contents.

   B. The fireproof filing cabinet and all of its contents.

   C. All of the money that was located in the safe, desk, and in the mobile home.

   D. All papers, tapes, and other documents of The House of Yahweh.

   These items listed above are property of The House of Yahweh, and were entrusted to our pastor and Overseer, Elder Yisrayl Hawkins. They were taken without the permission of either Elder Yisrayl Hawkins, or the body of Elders of The House of Yahweh. These must be returned immediately! Kay Hawkins, you are guilty of stealing according to the Laws of Yahweh.

   Kay Hawkins, to allow you to continue in your present actions would not show true love to you. We, as the body of Elders are sincerely praying to Yahweh that you will heed the words of the judgment and decision, that you will repent of your sins, and come back into unity with your husband, the body of Messiah, and The House of Yahweh.

   If you have any questions concerning the judgment and decision, you must contact Elder Shaul Schneider.

There were fifteen signatures on this document, Yisrayl Hawkins' among them. The letter that I had sent to Yisrayl on December 11, 1993, was finally answered by him on May 14, 1994, and was delivered by two of his lieutenants. Part of his response states,

Kallahyah, please repent. Return the money that belongs to Yahweh's work. I will always take care of you and the children.

The next day, May 15, 1994, I returned one safe and one fireproof letter file which had been in the feast trailer that Yisrayl had given to me; this was his half. I still had one more safe and one more letter file that had been in my house; this was my half. When I returned the first two items, I also submitted my resignation as the Secretary of the Corporation of The House of Yahweh. I stated,

> I have never stolen from The House of Yahweh in the past, and I will not steal from Yahweh, ever. As you can see, the safe and file have not been opened, so the contents there, whatever they are, is intact. As for the money in the desk, I am enclosing a copy of your letter, dated 2-24-1987, which authorized me that this is my money.

I also relinquished any claim to power or authority, real or implied. I also addressed the libel and slander focused against me and advised him to cease immediately.

I had not been to services that Sabbath, May 14, and the Feast of Pentecost was on May 17. The only way I could go back was to sign some vows.

As I was reading this in my current mental state, I asked myself, "Why would I have even wanted to go back?" Knowing what I know now, I would not have gone back to what had most certainly become, "The House of Hawkins."

At the time I made the decision, I knew that Yahweh and His Son were not there, but my children were; and I was not going to leave voluntarily.

Yisrayl created a document of "vows" for me to vow to and to sign. On May 16, 1994, in the evening, Elder Yeremyah Jeffries came to my house and gave me this document. As I read this, I realized that it was another trap. There was no way that I would be able to perform the words written upon this piece of paper. Yisrayl also knew that when I gave my word that I kept it.

Yeremyah asked me, "Have you read it?" I stated, "I have."

Yeremyah then asked me, "Do you vow to it?"

All I said was, "I know what it says."

A vow to Yahweh must be spoken aloud and given freely, without coercion. I did not say that I vowed to perform anything. My signature is on this piece of paper, and that is all that it is—a piece of paper.

The next day, May 17, 1994, was Pentecost, and I was stalked continuously. Yisrayl's guards positioned themselves around me as I sat in the sanctuary. If I had stood up and objected to what had been going on, they were trained, and instructed, to subdue me and bodily carry me from the building. I had witnessed others who had been treated in this way.

I remember that a bird flew into the sanctuary, just about the time that Yisrayl walked up to the podium. It started to fly from one end of the sanctuary to the other; flying around and around. According to old-wives-tales, this was a sign that a death in the family had occurred.

During this feast, a High Day, I later learned that Yisrayl's henchmen, his young, lust filled Elders, had summoned my son, Justin Hawkins, to a meeting. They tried to convince Justin to break his vow to me; the vow he made that he would not tell anyone where the safe and letter file were located, the two that I still had.

I made the mistake of letting Elder Bill Stubbs know where these were located in Abilene. The henchmen then got Bill Stubbs in their hands, on the Holy Day, and he broke under their relentless assault.

He told these men where they were located. On the same Holy Day, these men broke into my storage room in Abilene and stole the safe and letter file that I still had.

I was later informed that these Elders assured Justin that he was not to keep his vow to me. To Bill Stubbs' credit, he called me that same night and told me what had happened; he was very apologetic and filled with remorse.

Justin and I drove into Abilene. I was praying all the way that my valuable personal papers were still there. When we arrived, the lock was broken and the safe and letter file were missing. My valuable papers were still there. We retrieved what remained.

The next day, May 18, 1994, Justin and I rented a large safety deposit box at a local bank, and in it we placed all of my important papers, the money, gold, silver, and the guns which had been in my house.

Justin was later accused of stealing $250,000.00 from The House of Yahweh, which he most certainly did not, but this accusation focused attention on Justin rather than on Yisrayl Hawkins, the real guilty party.

When we returned in the afternoon on this date, I found a letter from Yisrayl on my desk in the living room. Many protestations of love were written therein, hollow words with no emotion. The truth was that he wanted me back to perform the writing, typesetting, and every other responsibility which would make the façade of The House of Yahweh to continue to appear righteous.

Later that week I heard a noise; someone was at the front of my house. The men in a pickup were driving off as I came out of the door. There, rolled out onto my carport were the empty safes and letter files. This was a childish maneuver, but typical. This was Yisrayl's way of gloating. I placed these in my house and still use them today.

On Sabbath, May 21, 1994, I received another letter from Yisrayl Hawkins. The rationale within begins to show his actual mindset,

My Dearest

Is it not strang (sic) that our son Dennis refused children because of the tie-down.

It did the same for us. We must have put this in his mind as a child when he saw how this also tied his family down.

Alex Joseph told me this was one of the things his wives praised, because each of them could be free any time they wanted to be.

Yahweh laws could have freed us years ago...

A cord of 3, 4 or more is not easily broken. Its (sic) very benefishal (sic) & joyous to all those who would come away from their selfish way to life, to a house built without hands. Love-true love, Y.H.

True love, according to Yisrayl Hawkins' interpretation, is cult lingo for "keeping every law." I received several more letters afterward, each proclaiming "love, true love," and all the time that he was writing them he was taking everything of value from my farm that could be carried off. The road to my farm was open, and Yisrayl's men could come in at any time. He wanted everything.

The last straw was when he decided to take the two best tractors and the three best pieces of farm equipment from me. It was dusk on

Friday, June 24, 1994, the beginning of the Sabbath. My children and I were visiting on the patio after our Sabbath dinner. Then one of my sons said, "What is that?" I heard the sound of tractors, and when I looked to the north I saw my tractors and farm equipment being driven across my field toward Highway 603.

I immediately got into my 1982 Cadillac, drove over to the highway, and blocked the gate with my car, just as they drove up. Robert Mosheh and Robert's son were driving the tractors, and one of the mentally-handicapped men, who lived on Highway 603, was riding on one of the pieces of farm equipment.

I told them I was calling the sheriff to have them arrested for theft. When the sheriff's deputy arrived, Yisrayl Hawkins had already contacted the sheriff's office and advised that it was he who ordered my equipment taken; that these men were acting on his behalf. I asked the sheriff's deputy to write down the makes, models, and serial numbers of everything there. He completed this documentation, signed and dated it, and gave this to me. If he had not done this, there would have been no way to have proven that these pieces of equipment had ever been on my farm.

Now, I knew that if I did not file for divorce and lock my place down, that there would be absolutely nothing left of any value; especially when that Sunday, June 26, there an unsuccessful attempt made to take the valuable welding equipment.

On Monday, June 27, 1994, I went to the bank where Yisrayl and I had our joint accounts. I had our new credit card and I withdrew $4,500.00 in cash. Afterward, I went to see my attorney and filed for divorce.

Yisrayl was served divorce papers, filed in Taylor County, on Tuesday morning, June 28, 1994. Yisrayl immediately pleaded that he lived in Callahan County, so the first papers filed were not valid. I immediately instructed my attorneys to file in Callahan County, and these were also processed on Tuesday, June 28, 1994.

Yisrayl hired two attorneys, one to represent him and another to represent The House of Yahweh. Justin and his wife and I were served with Respondents' Original Answer, hand delivered by the deputy of the court on June 28, 1994, at 6:20 pm. This document stated that,

Respondent (Yisrayl Hawkins) believes there is a reasonable

expectation of reconciliation and pleads "condonation"[33] to the actions complained of by Petitioner (Kay Hawkins).

This same date, the morning of June 28, I went to a hardware business in Abilene, purchased sections of brass chain and large padlocks, and chained and locked every entrance to my farm. It was virtually impossible to cut these chains and padlocks without huge bolt-cutters or a cutting torch. No one would be getting onto my farm now, unless he or she had a key.

When Yisrayl saw the chains and locks, he knew that I meant business when I filed for divorce. There certainly was neither reconciliation nor "condonation" for him to look forward to.

Hawkins' attorneys filed An Amended Temporary Restraining Order and Order Setting Hearing for Temporary Orders on June 29, 1994. These were hand-delivered to me, and also to Justin and his wife, by the Deputy of the Court, accompanied by Elder Shaul Schneider. These were delivered to us on Friday, July 1, 1994, at 7:00 pm. Later, on this same Sabbath night, each of us received another letter, hand-delivered at 11:00 pm,

Kay Hawkins. This letter is to notify you that you have been excommunicated from The House of Yahweh, effective July 1, 1994.

The grounds for excommunication were that I had taken a stand against the established doctrines and the body of Elders. This letter continued,

Only a letter of reinstatement, signed by the Overseer of The House of Yahweh, which may be issued upon your bringing forth fruits of repentance, will be able to supersede this letter of expulsion.

However, we highly recommend that you find and join a church. It is evident from your rejection of the sound doctrine of The House of Yahweh that a church would better suit your personality and satisfy your whims. In Yahshua's Name

33 Condonation, in law, an express or implied forgiving by the husband or wife of the other's adultery.

This was signed by twelve of the youngest, most gullible, easily deceived, lust-filled, so-called Elders. Yisrayl Hawkins didn't even have the courage to sign it. No older and wiser men had put their names on this document, because they had already left. On Sunday, July 10, 1994, Yisrayl sent another "love" note to "help you get back into the H.O.Y. where you and I both can work together..."

On Monday, July 11, I received a copy of Yisrayl's book, *Reconsidering Yahweh's Laws of Slavery and Marriage Obligations.* The inscription inside this book reads,

> On this the eve of the New Moon 7-11-94, I give this, my latest book to my wife Kallahyah Hawkins, in hopes this writing will once again renew the Spirit of Yahweh in her, bringing to remembrance her vows to me and to Yahweh, vows that bind us together forever as man and wife. Yahweh joined us together. What Yahweh joins together, let not man put asunder. With love, true love, (signed) Yisrayl Hawkins

On Monday afternoon, July 11, 1994, I received an unexpected phone call from Yisrayl Hawkins. The conversation began with Yisrayl saying, "Tell me what you want..."

This was the same line that he used on everyone in order to bribe them. Those who took the bait came under his absolute control. I told him that I wanted him to repent of the sins that he had committed, and return to The Faith.

The only other phone call that he made to me was after our divorce was final in December of 1994; he wanted to know if I would like to invest as a partner in the mobile home park that he had just purchased.

I was not the only person who was excommunicated on July 1, 1994. There were several, Justin and his wife included. There were more than fifty members who left The House of Yahweh at the same time. Some had excommunication papers, most of them did not. These ex-members and I met together for the first time on the Sabbath, July 2, 1994.

During one of our later meetings we learned that the members of The House of Yahweh were pinning their ears to the door in order to become Yisrayl's slaves forever. Afterward we heard that Satan was a woman.

With the $4,500.00 that I had gotten from our credit card before

I filed for divorce, I purchased a used car, a red Nissan, for Justin and his wife.

It was on Monday, November 29, 1993, that DeeDee was driving Justin's pickup over to Yahweh Village. She was taking one of Yisrayl's workers back home. Justin's wife was with them. DeeDee turned off of Highway 603, into the entrance of the road which leads to the school inside the property. Just as DeeDee turned right and started to enter, Justin's wife screamed. DeeDee immediately stopped.

A large dually pickup had veered off the highway, drove through the yard, and rammed into the side of the pickup, just in front of the passenger cab. The engine was crushed as Justin's pickup was slammed sideways. Dee said that if she had not stopped, the pickup would have rammed directly into Justin's wife. Thankfully, no one was severely injured, but the pickup was a total loss.

Justin had been making truck and insurance payments to Yisrayl for this truck. When it was totaled, Yisrayl collected the insurance money because the truck title and insurance were still in his name.

Yisrayl did not pay Justin for his truck nor did he replace it. Justin and his wife and baby were now getting rides from me, from his sister, DeeDee, or from one their friends. Yisrayl owed them this car because he had kept all the insurance money for himself.

Yisrayl claimed that everything he owned was on the farm; he didn't have anything else.

I was ordered to make a full accounting of everything that I had. I began a complete inventory of my farm, and on July 28, 1994, I found "bugging" devices attached to my phone line: one voice activated telephone recording control and one voice activated cassette tape recorder. I still have these items.

When I did some research at the Abilene County Clerk's office, I found that Justin Hawkins and Yisrayl Hawkins had purchased a large, expensive home on Lake Fort Phantom Hill, at #2 Angels Breath Road. When I asked Justin about this, he said that Yisrayl called him into his office and instructed him to sign some papers, which he did. Justin said he didn't know what they were. One of these papers was evidently a Power of Attorney; after the divorce was final, ownership of this house reverted to Yisrayl's name only. Yisrayl purchased another house at 410 Grape Street in Abilene, another at 350 Seminole. I can only guess about the other properties that he had purchased behind my back. If he had hidden behind Justin when he purchased this house on Angels Breath Road, how many others were phantom owners of Yisrayl's real estate?

I realized the futility of trying to find out. I did not have the money to pursue his real estate ventures. Therefore, in the divorce I asked for my farm and home place and half of the rental property which had not been deeded over to The House of Yahweh throughout the years.

It was also ordered on July 28, 1994, that DeeDee become the temporary Court Appointed Trustee of the accounts for AAA Mobile Home Park, our business. She was to collect rents, create accountings, and split the receipts between Yisrayl and me. By my estimate, I was due to receive over $11,000 in September of 1994.

Elder Shaul Schneider had volunteered to collect the rents for DeeDee, because all of our renters were members of The House of Yahweh. Elder Shaul Schneider stated to DeeDee that everyone was behind on their rent. I never did get my part.

In October, 1994, I went to see Dad in Royston, Texas. We drove to the cemetery in Roby and visited Mother, who had died in 1980, and my brother, Rodney, who had died in 1991. We also visited my grandmother and granddaddy Polk in the same cemetery. We then drove to Jayton, Texas, and visited Daddy's side of the family in the cemetery there. I was beginning to reconnect with my real family, with the living and those who were already asleep.

The months leading up to the date that our divorce was finalized, on December 9, 1994, were also filled with pathetic passive-aggressive maneuvers meant to demoralize and intimidate me. I knew all of Yisrayl's henchmen were cowards; I knew Yisrayl was a coward. Everything they did to me and my farm was performed in the dark. At the time, I had the greatest contempt for them.

I was awarded my home, farm, farm equipment and some cattle, a 1982 Cadillac sedan and the 1979 Ford pickup, one small mobile home, with four rent houses in Abilene—half of all that remained of all the lands and property we had deeded over to The House of Yahweh throughout our marriage. I received the contents of the desk that we had cleaned out. I was awarded the complete Library and barely enough money to build up my own small, successful rent business.

After Shaul Schneider came to my house and retrieved Yisrayl's guns and all of the documents and files that Yisrayl Hawkins wanted, everything that remained in my house and in my possession was declared to be mine, by decree of the court.

The day that my divorce was final, marked the day that their open harassment against me ceased. The documents were signed and sealed. I was forty-five-years old, and finally free at last from the oppression and control of Yisrayl Bill Hawkins.

CHAPTER NINETEEN

1995 Through 2011
Mental Recovery and The Real World

The hard physical labor involved in building up my rent business was actually part of my psychiatric therapy. However, I could not have had a successful business without the help of my friends, a man and his wife, who worked for me until I sold my farm properties in 2006.

Another part of my psychiatric therapy was taking care of my small cattle herd, and caring for my two grandchildren. This was the only psychiatric therapy which was able to help me. No one knows what it felt like to be involved in what The House of Yahweh had slowly become, unless they had experienced the same thing. I and everyone else who had left were the veterans who had survived the spiritual warfare waged by Yisrayl Bill Hawkins against The House of Yahweh. There was no Ph.D. in this area who would be able to understand and help.

Before my divorce was final, the older, wiser Elders tried to help all of us who had come out of The House of Yahweh, bruised and battered. In September, 1994, they wrote five articles in a newsletter, entitled, *The True House, Where is it?* These five men, wise and knowledgeable, had stated to Yisrayl Hawkins that they would not do to their wives what he had done to me. Since they were not "loyal" to Yisrayl Hawkins, they could not remain.

I was still so mentally dysfunctional at the time that I still could not accept the fact that Yisrayl Hawkins was not one of "The Two Witnesses."

It would still be several more years before I would recover completely from the mind-control and manipulation, with its "black and white" thinking.[34] I believe that I was experiencing the symptoms of post traumatic stress syndrome, since I felt intense anger; it was as though I had been confined in a concentration camp against my will.[35]

I was so grateful that so many of my friends and family had come out with me. I was not cast out by myself. I believe that we gave each other mental support; we understood each other perfectly. I cannot imagine how it would have felt if I had no emotional and spiritual support at all.

I would later learn that Yisrayl Hawkins had appointed Paul Raymond Schneider as his agent by Statutory Durable Power of Attorney, with Donald Michel Sheets as his successor. Yisrayl had also appointed "her" as his agent by the same Statutory Durable Power of Attorney, with Bruce Edward Bowler as "her" successor. These Public Records were signed March 25, 1995.

Afterward, I was contacted by almost every member who left The House of Yahweh. They wanted answers to their questions, which I gave to them. I also intervened in a child custody case in which one parent was in The House of Yahweh and the other parent was never a member. The parent in The House of Yahweh did not get custody.

I also began to understand how someone could have the capability of being completely inhuman to another person; how someone could openly affirm "love, true love" to me, while at the same time brutally assaulting my emotions and feelings. I came to understand that only a person who has a personality disorder has this capacity.

I learned that, "...psychopaths do not tell you their "plans" are completely provisional, improvised and subject to change in an instant and without any prior warning...It is just one rush to the next, then they become bored and move on to the next...to manipulate,

---

34 *Take Back Your Life Recovering from Cults and Abusive Relationships,* Janja Lalich and Madeleine Tobias, "The Poverty of Black and White Thinking," page 112; "Black and White Thinking," pages 118-119; the paragraph entitled, "All-or-nothing thinking," page 113.

35 *Take Back Your Life,* Lalich and Tobias, pages 320-321.

exploit, and eventually ruin...A psychopath goes through life leaving a trail of used-up victims, broken hearts, financial ruin, shattered hopes, destroyed organizations...as well as a plethora of unfulfilled promises in their wake, and all this will be carried out by the psychopath without any consideration for consequences or moral responsibility."[36]

I learned that a psychopath is "...a child, sometimes even a quite bright child, of eight, nine, or ten, who has outgrown the...world of early childhood, but who has not yet grown into the...state common to adolescence...We find a child, with the body and age of an adolescent or adult, living unprotected from the extraordinary vulnerabilities of his ordinary mental limitations. No 10-year-old is equipped to handle either the freedoms or responsibilities of adult life."[37]

I learned that psychopaths, also known as sociopaths, "...are bystanders to the emotional lives of others... envious and scornful of feelings they cannot have or understand...sociopaths are cold, with shallow emotions, and they live in a dark world of their own...He can witness or order acts of utter brutality without experiencing a shred of emotion. He casts himself in a role of total control, which he plays to the hilt...What is most promised in cults—peace, joy, enlightenment, love, and security—are goals that are forever out of the leader's reach, and thus also the followers. Because the leader is not genuine, neither are his promises."[38]

When I understood all these things, I finally began to understand how Yisrayl Hawkins' juvenile, emotionally-immature, mind functioned—in a cold, calculated pattern of initial idealization, accompanied by compliments, charm, and flattery; gradual devaluation, accompanied by verbal insults and criticism; then destruction of the project, accompanied by abandonment. If the

---

36 *Puzzling People, the labyrinth of the psychopath,* Copyright © MMXI Thomas Sheridan, published by Velluminous Press, www.vellumious.com, pages 30, 97, 33.

37 *Unmasking the Psychopath, Antisocial Personality and Related Syndromes,* Copyright © 1986 by William H. Reid, Darwin Dorr, John I. Walker, Jack W. Bonner, from Chapter Three, *The Child Behind the Mask: Sociopathy as Developmental Delay,* by Robert G. Kegan, page 75, published by W.W. Norton & Company, 500 5th Avenue, New York, NY 10110, used with permission.

38 *Take Back Your Life,* Janja Lalich and Madeleine Tobias, "Shallow Emotions," page 63.

"project" was a human being, the destruction was also accompanied by a smear campaign launched against the discarded victim.[39]

"We must, never let it be forgotten, judge a man by his actions, rather than by his words." [40]

Learning all these things helped me to mentally recover from the physical, mental, and spiritual abuse that I had suffered throughout the years. I also began to understand why Yisrayl Hawkins continuously made the immature, selfish, destructive decisions that he did, why he was such an irresponsible parent, why he decided that only he had the right to rule The House of Yahweh, and then to destroy it by turning it into a polygamous doomsday slave compound—and how he did it.

In December, 1995, I decided to get a face-lift. Emotionally, this gave me back ten years of my life; at the time I physically began to feel much younger.

I also wanted to get rid of the 1982 Cadillac that was given to me in 1994 by Yisrayl Hawkins. It was already twelve years old when I received it, and it was a dinosaur and a gas hog. I purchased a used, red Buick Regal, which was a very reliable, comfortable car; it was also rather sporty looking.

In January, 1996, I learned that members of The House of Yahweh were changing their last names to "Hawkins." This information was front page news in the January 21, 1996, issue of *The Abilene Reporter News*, written by Richard Horn and Loretta Fulton, Staff Writers.

I thought to myself, "Of course, with all of those poor little illegitimate babies being born out there now, this is just another manipulation to make it easier to register these babies' birth certificates. Their last names would all be Hawkins, instead of Father Unknown."

The *Texas Monthly* Magazine, January 1997, page 115, gave Yisrayl the *Bum Steer Award* for not responding to their telephone calls about the name changes, "Mr. Hawkins Could Not (89 times) Be Reached for Comment."

Well, with news like this, the media was requesting more information. Another article entitled, *Sect stores treasures on earth*, was published in

---

39 *Puzzling People, the labyrinth of the psychopath*, Thomas Sheridan, page 39 under "History of Brief or Failed Relations Ending Badly," and page 40 "Idealisation Followed by Cold Rejection."

40 *The Mask of Sanity* by Hervey Cleckley, Fifth Edition, Copyright © 1988 by Emily S. Cleckley, page 348.

the Sunday, February 18, 1996, issue of *The Abilene Reporter News,* also written by Richard Horn and Loretta Fulton.

My son-in-law called me that morning, and said, "Kay, how could you?!" I said, "How could I do what?" He said, "How could you have given such an interview?"

When I read this article, I learned that it was me who was supposed to have given the interview, and to have vehemently denied that our 1994 divorce was based on Yisrayl's affairs and his practice of polygamy.

Since it was not me who granted the telephone interview with the reporters, I called the newspaper and informed them about it. On Tuesday, February 20, 1996, Richard Horn and Loretta Fulton wrote the front page article, *Ex-wife: I didn't give the interview; ex-wife of religious sect's leader says impostor was quoted in Sunday's story.*

This opened the door for me to go public with the information which I had, which also helped me to psychologically heal. The articles written by Richard Horn and Loretta Fulton evidently were dispersed throughout Texas. Evan Moore came to Abilene on a fact finding mission. The result was an extensive article written by him for *The Houston Chronicle,* Sunday, March 24, 1996, beginning on the front page, entitled, *A House Divided; Tensions tear at polygamous Abilene-area cult.*

The *Texas Monthly,* July 1997, pages 74–81, printed an extensive article about The House of Yahweh, Yisrayl Hawkins, and me. The front cover of this magazine proclaimed, *Abilene's House of Yahweh believes… Satan is a woman, the Pope is her puppet, and the world will end in three years. Inside a doomsday cult,* by Robert Draper.

The *Abilene Reporter News* published a follow-up about the *Texas Monthly* article in the Friday, June 27, 1997, issue on page 5A, written by Anthony Wilson, Staff Writer. I stated in this article,

"It's my prayer the House of Yahweh one day will return to the purpose of serving the creator and not the man."

Thereafter, between 1996 and 2008, I made several media appearances, among them, 20/20 on the ABC Television Network, in a segment of Strange Universe, with studios located in Burbank, California, in two stories aired on WXYZ Television in Southfield, Michigan, in a segment on the A&E Television Channel, entitled,

Mind Control, on ABC News, and on the *Dr Phil Show,* taped in Los Angeles, California.

I was told by my Tax Lady that the Internal Revenue Audit in 1993 and my divorce in 1994 were the best things that could have happened to me. If the audit had taken place at any time after this date that I would have been implicated if any arrears had been found. Yes, I believe that Yahweh protected me and that He granted me freedom and mental recovery.

However, I would have preferred that the Internal Revenue Service have audited the financial records of The House of Yahweh organization itself. I have been advised that this would be an infringement of the Constitution.

Every organization in this world has a historical beginning. The House of Yahweh ultimately had its beginning with the First Amendment to the Constitution of The United States of America which instituted the separation of Church and State, citing "Congress shall make no law respecting an establishment of religion, or prohibiting the free exercise thereof."

Without the express protection bestowed by The Internal Revenue Service of the United States of America directly upon Non-Profit 501(c)(3) Religious Organizations, The House of Yahweh, known as the largest doomsday cult in America today, simply would not be allowed to exist.

I believe the First Amendment should be amended. A law should be enacted to prevent self serving cult leaders from gaining complete control over the money that comes in. Checks and balances should be enacted in every non-profit organization, including Non-Profit 501(c)(3) organizations.

Power corrupts; absolute power corrupts absolutely. [41]

Robert J. Lifton in his article, *The Appeal of the Death Trip,* which appeared in *The New York Times* on January 7, 1979, explains the definition of a "cult" as opposed to a "religion,"

> I tend to speak of cults in terms of a cluster of groups that, for the sake of definition, have certain characteristics: First, a

---

41 John Emerich Edward Dalberg Acton, first Baron Acton (1834–1902), wrote this opinion in a letter to Bishop Mandell Creighton in 1887.

charismatic leader who…increasingly becomes the object of worship. Spiritual ideas of a more general kind are likely to give way to worship of the person of the leader.

Second, a series of processes that can be associated with what has been called "coercive persuasion" or "thought reform."

A third characteristic of what I am calling cults has to do with the tendency toward manipulation from above…with exploitation—economic, sexual, or other—of often genuine seekers who bring idealism from below…"[42]

When The House of Yahweh first started, it was not a "cult" which focused its worship on a charismatic leader—but it became this way.

When The House of Yahweh first started, it was not a "cult" which began to control almost every aspect of its members' lives—but it became this way.

When The House of Yahweh first started, there was no manipulation from above, with exploitation of genuine seekers who brought idealism from below—but it became this way.

And when The House of Yahweh became the haven of a "cult" which focused adoration, money, and absolute power and control upon one mortal, human man, Yisrayl Bill Hawkins—it turned against the principles upon which its Non-Profit 501(c)(3) Status was obtained.

Something should change. Either The House of Yahweh should return to the Founding Principles upon which its Non-Profit 501(c)(3) Status was obtained, or The House of Yahweh should relinquish its Non-Profit 501(c)(3) Status.

The people of the United States of America are being cheated out of millions of dollars in tax revenue simply because these types of cult leaders cannot be held accountable for their despicable, greedy, self-serving actions.

---

42 From *The New York Times,* January 7, © 1979 The New York Times. All rights reserved. Used by permission and protected by the Copyright Laws of the United States. The printing, copying, redistribution, or retransmission of the content without express written permission is prohibited.

When this type of cult leader is fiscally restrained, he or she quickly loses interest in "non-profit" enterprises.

When I finally started to overcome mentally, I began to think about my future. There is no such thing as a "Retirement Plan" or "Major Medical Insurance" in The House of Yahweh, so I decided to return to work in December of 1998. I began to work for a major corporation in the year 2000 and retired after eleven years of service there.

How am I today? I am at peace. I have my children, grandchildren, great-grandchildren, and a best friend in my close circle of everyday life. I have problems, just like everyone else, but I have my health and I love my family. I also love Yahweh and Yahshua. My cup is full.

Afterword

If you are thinking about leaving a situation like I was in—or have already left—but feel hopeless about surviving on the "outside," I recommend that you read *Take Back Your Life, Recovering from Cults and Abusive Relationships,* ©1994, 2006 by Janja Lalich and Madeleine Tobias, Bay Tree Publishing, 721 Creston Road, Berkeley, CA 94708.

Take Back Your Life, Recovering from Cults and Abusive Relationships, is the Second Edition of their work, revised and expanded. Some material in this book was originally published as *Captive Hearts, Captive Minds, Freedom and Recovery from Cults and Abusive Relationships* by Janja Lalich and Madeleine Tobias in 1994—which gave me the answers I was searching for at the time.

I also recommend that you read *Puzzling People, the labyrinth of the psychopath,* by Thomas Sheridan, Copyright ©MMXI, published by Velluminous Press. This book describes the common, everyday psychopaths who surround us; how to recognize them, and how to avoid them or minimize their influence.

Both of these books are written in plain English, and contain excellent advice, references, and resources, to which I will refer you.

If you want to learn more about Yisrayl Hawkins and how he has affected other ex-members, along with other interesting information, go to the website, www.themanbehindthename.com.

I am on Facebook and Twitter, and I invite you to visit me. You may also write me at: PO Box 921, Abilene, Texas 79604-0921.

Appendix One

Genealogy
The Fruit Doesn't Fall Far From the Tree

Over the years Buffalo Bill Hawkins, now known as Yisrayl Bill Hawkins, has created a persona that he and his families are Jewish, thereby embellishing his credibility as a religious leader. On the back cover of one of his books he actually makes the statement that his parents were Jewish, who escaped from Europe and settled in the United States for safety. He did not state what year this might have been. If this was a true statement, his ancestors had to have arrived long before the Civil War, because they completely assimilated into Southern Confederate sympathizers who made their way to Texas, and there was not one Jewish custom practiced along the way. On every United States Census Bill's ancestors are listed as being farmers, some owning land and some sharecropping for others.

Hawkins

Bill's Great-Great-Grandfather on the Hawkins side of the family was Henry George Hawkins, b. September 17, 1790–d. October 27, 1862, in Denton, Texas, who was married to Nancy James b. 1792–d. 1876. The Hawkins family can trace their ancestry back to John Hawkins, who was born November 14, 1680, in Plymouth, England, who arrived in Maryland in 1694. Prior to this, the Hawkins had a distinguished history in England. One of his ancestors, William Amadas Hawkins, was an officer in the navy of King Henry VIII, and was Lord of the Manor of Sutton Valetort.

Bill's Great-Grandfather was William Martin Hawkins, born January 15, 1839, in Barren, Kentucky, Barren County, who died August 20, 1871, in Little Elm, Denton County, Texas. William Martin married Sarah Elizabeth Jane Rue on February 2, 1862. Bill's Great-Grandmother, Sarah Jane Rue Hawkins, was born February 2, 1841, in Longwood, Missouri, Pettis County. She died on August 26, 1920, in Denton, Texas, Denton County. She was listed on the 1880 United States Census as Sarah Stapp, Age 39 and head of the family living in Denton County, Texas.

Buffalo Bill's Grandfather was Lewis Daniel Hawkins, born January 19, 1870 in Texas. Lewis Daniel's first wife was Molly Amanda Payne Hawkins, born August 2, 1877, in Denton, Texas, whom he married on October 15, 1893, and with whom he had Daniel and Rachel. After her death on April 15, 1898, Lewis Daniel married Flora Bell Earles Hawkins on August 10, 1898. Flora Bell was born May 21, 1880, in Salem, Missouri, Dent County. She died July 29, 1964, in Denton, Texas, Denton County. Flora Bell's father, William Pleasant Earles, was born February 12, 1848, in the State of Virginia, and died December 18, 1901, in Earlsboro, Oklahoma, Pottawatomie County. Flora Bell's mother was Virginia Ladd, who was born in 1848 in Tullahoma, Tennessee, Coffee County, and died February 4, 1883, in Whitehorse, Oklahoma, Woods County. Virginia Ladd's family traces to her grandfather, John Ladd, who was born in 1630 in Norfolk County, Virginia. Lewis Daniel and Flora Bell's first son was William Otis Hawkins, Buffalo Bill's father, who was born April 11, 1902, in Texas.

Russell

Bill's Grandfather on his mother's side of the family was Pearl E. Russel, located on the 1910 United States Census in Justice Precinct 3, Tarrant County, Texas, District 160, age 31, and born in 1879 in Tennessee. Both of Pearl's parents were born in Tennessee. Bill's maternal Grandmother was Susie White Russel, age 29, born in 1881 in Kentucky. Both Susie's parents were born in Kentucky.

Maggie Mae Russell, Bill's Mother, was born July 7, 1904 in Texas.

The 1920 United States Census shows that Bill's Maternal Grandfather was a Widower living in Justice Precinct 2, Rains County, Emory, Texas, and was going by the name of L.E. Russle, age 47, born about 1873. Susie White Russell died sometime between April 1914 and the 1920 Census, which was taken on June 16, 1920. Susie White Russell was between the ages of 33 to 38 at her death. Maggie Mae Russle was age 15 in the 1920 Census; Odus Hawkins was 17.

The 1930 United States Census shows that William Otis was age 22 and Maggie Mae was age 17 when they were married around 1922. Their oldest son, J.G. Hawkins, was born September 11, 1924, in Rains County, Emory, Texas.

The 1930 United States Census shows Maggie's father was living in Precinct 1, Young County, Graham, Texas, and then was going by the name of Purre E. Russell, age 60, born about 1870, and was listed as married to Millie Russell, age 55.

Pearle E, L.E.(P.E), or Purre E. Russell did not seem to know when he was actually born. Was it 1870, 1873, or 1879?

William Otis and Maggie were also living in Justice Precinct 1, Young County, Graham, Texas, in 1930.

William Otis Hawkins Born April 11, 1902–Died Sept 6, 1974
    Married Maggie Mae Russell
    Born July 7, 1904–Died Feb 20, 1956
Both buried in Tonk Valley Cemetery, Graham, Texas.

There were seven children born to them during their marriage:

J.G Hawkins Born September 11, 1924, Emory, Texas Rains Co.
    Died March 22, 1991, Odessa, Texas
    Married Isabel on June 2, 1944,
    Born June 2, 1927–Died Feb 11, 2005
Both buried in Sunset Memorial Gardens, Odessa, Texas

Mary Belle Hawkins Born Dec 15, 1926–Died Jan 12, 1929
    Buried in Medlan Chapel Cemetery, Graham, Texas

Margaret Hawkins Followwill
    Born May 5, 1929–Died July 22, 1993

Vernon George (Sonny) Hawkins
    Born Oct 20, 1930–Died June 1, 1955
    Buried in Tonk Valley Cemetery, Graham, Texas

Buffalo Bill Hawkins Born August 28, 1934, Lexington, Oklahoma

Texas James Hawkins Born Oct 29, 1940–Died Feb 6, 2006

Gene Truman Hawkins Born April 9, 1945–Died Nov 25, 2011

J.G. and Buffalo Bill Hawkins 1963-1969

It was around the middle of 1963, that J.G. Hawkins and family moved to Romney, Texas, located on the highway between Cisco and Rising Star. Voy Wilks, director and overseer of the Church of God, Seventh Day, had heard J.G. preach on a local radio station. Voy drove to Graham, Texas, and offered J.G. Hawkins the position of pastor of this congregation, which he accepted. J.G. preached every Sabbath Day and preferred to preach about the Great Tribulation and the Place of Safety in Israel.

Early in 1965, Bill and his family moved to Cross Plains, Texas, to be close to his brother. By the time Bill and family arrived, J.G and Voy had already parted company. Voy and his family were no longer meeting with the Church of God, Seventh Day, and J.G. Hawkins. This is why the Assembly of Yahweh, 7th Day, was never religiously affiliated with The House of Yahweh or Bill Hawkins.

It was reported that Bill, when he occasionally attended services with his family, would open a copy of *The Plain Truth* published by Herbert W. Armstrong's Worldwide Church of God, and read it instead of listening to J.G.'s sermons. Bill and his family would move to Abilene, Texas, in the spring of 1967.

When members Don and Mary Montgomery sold their farm, they gave a tenth of their proceeds to J.G. and moved to Israel to be safe from the Great Tribulation. Don and Mary finally settled at Moshav Be'er Tuvia in Israel.

It was also in Romney, Texas, that J.G. began another affair, this time with a married woman in the congregation. He had already left behind a daughter by another girlfriend in Oklahoma. His girlfriend from the Romney congregation had recently received a sizable inheritance from her mother. With his new girlfriend's inheritance money, and with the tithe that he had received from the Montgomery family, J.G. set out in 1969 to move to Israel with his wife, Isabel, and three of their four children; with his brother Texas James and his wife and children; and with his girlfriend and her daughter.

J.G. and Isabel's oldest son decided that he wasn't going to Israel with them. Isabel said this caused her to be severely grieved, especially when J.G. turned his back on him and refused to have anything else to do with him at the time.

The group went to Israel as tourists, going to Canada, London, Switzerland, Germany, Greece, and Turkey and spending quite a lot of unnecessary money. Isabel said J.G. went to a travel agency to book their trip, but the agent sent them all over the world instead of directly to their destination. On reflection, this was meant to be because during the trip J.G. was confronted by Turkish visa authorities, and was challenged about his name which was only initials. It was during that confrontation that J.G. said to "call me Jacob."

The group rode a bus to Istanbul, Turkey, caught a ferry, and finally arrived in Israel by bus. They settled in Kibbutz Ir'ovot, a farming commune created by a polygamist named Sandy, who had two wives.

Isabel told me while they were at Ir'ovot, that J.G., now Jacob-Yaacov, planned to go with his girlfriend to the marriage license bureau, swear that he was not married to anyone else and that his girlfriend's husband had died, so that he could marry her.

Isabel told me that she went to Sandy, the leader of Ir'ovot, and told him that Jacob's girlfriend was still a married woman. Sandy told Jacob that he could not get married to a married woman, that it was adultery. It was her daughter who challenged Jacob, saying, "How can you marry my mother when my daddy is still alive?" Isabel said it was Jacob's girlfriend's daughter who informed the Israeli Authorities of his plan.

Since polygamy is against the law in Israel, and because it is also illegal to get married to a married woman, Jacob was not allowed to get married to his girlfriend. After this, his girlfriend and her daughter returned to the States, and moved back into to her living husband's home.

Jacob, Isabel, and children left Kibbutz Ir'ovot and moved to Nazareth. Jacob wrote this account in *The Prophetic Watchman,* March/April, 1975, Vol. 2 No. 7,

> In the Fall of 1969, I and a little group went to Israel and settled in the Wilderness of Paran…lived there (Ir'ovot) nine months then went to Nazareth and attended an Ulpan to learn Hebrew.

This would have been between June and August of 1970. They moved to Block 750, Apt 30, Nazareth, Illit, Israel, where Isabel became employed as an inspector in a clothing manufacturing company, excelling in her position, while Jacob stayed at home, writing *The Prophetic Watchman* and sending it to the few people on his mailing list. Isabel also said that Jacob drank excessively and cried, blaming her for losing his girlfriend.

Tex and his family moved back to the United States in 1974, staying in Cross Plains for a short time before moving to Atlanta, Texas. Jacob and his family would return to the United States in 1975.

Endnotes

Chapter One

1. *The Prophetic Word* Magazine is *A HOUSE OF YAHWEH®TM Publication, Published by* THE HOUSE OF YAHWEH P.O. BOX 2498, Abilene, Texas 79604, 325-672-5420.

2. These Books, published by The House of Yahweh, were copyrighted between 1986 and 1993.

3. *The Encyclopedia Britannica,* published in the United States and Canada by Encyclopaedia Britannica, Inc., 331 North La Salle Street, Chicago, IL 60654-2682.

Chapter Nine

1. *Strong's Exhaustive Concordance,* Copyright 1890, by James Strong, Madison, N.J., Forty-Fourth Printing, 1986, Reprinted by Baker Book House, Grand Rapids, Michigan, *Hebrew Dictionary,* page 53.

2. *The Holy Name Bible,* Revised by A.B. Traina, Copyright 1963 by The Scripture Research Association, Inc., 14410 South Springfield Road, Brandywine, Maryland 20613, 1978, page 850.

3. *The Holy Name Bible,* A.B. Traina, page 903.

4. *The National Enquirer,* American Media, Inc., 4 New York Plaza, New York, New York, 10004.

Chapter Eleven

1. Ibid. *The Holy Name Bible,* A.B. Traina

2. *The Book of Yahweh,* Copyright 1987 by The House of Yahweh, Abilene, Texas; Yisrayl Hawkins, Elder and Overseer, First Printing.

3. *The Book of Yahweh,* Copyright 1988 by Yisrayl Hawkins, Elder and Overseer of The House of Yahweh, Abilene, Texas. Second Printing.

Chapter Twelve

1. Romans 16:7, Junia, wife of Andronicus. Both were Apostles. *The Anchor Bible, Romans: a new translation with introduction and commentary,* Joseph A. Fitzmyer, First Edition, Copyright 1993 by Doubleday, a division of Bantam Doubleday Dell Publishing Group, Inc., 1540 Broadway, New York, N.Y. 10036. Volume 33, pages 733-734.